C-1394   CAREER EXAMINATION SERIES

This is your
PASSBOOK for...

Power Distribution Maintainer

Test Preparation Study Guide
Questions & Answers

COPYRIGHT NOTICE

This book is SOLELY intended for, is sold ONLY to, and its use is RESTRICTED to individual, bona fide applicants or candidates who qualify by virtue of having seriously filed applications for appropriate license, certificate, professional and/or promotional advancement, higher school matriculation, scholarship, or other legitimate requirements of education and/or governmental authorities.

This book is NOT intended for use, class instruction, tutoring, training, duplication, copying, reprinting, excerption, or adaptation, etc., by:

1) Other publishers
2) Proprietors and/or Instructors of "Coaching" and/or Preparatory Courses
3) Personnel and/or Training Divisions of commercial, industrial, and governmental organizations
4) Schools, colleges, or universities and/or their departments and staffs, including teachers and other personnel
5) Testing Agencies or Bureaus
6) Study groups which seek by the purchase of a single volume to copy and/or duplicate and/or adapt this material for use by the group as a whole without having purchased individual volumes for each of the members of the group
7) Et al.

Such persons would be in violation of appropriate Federal and State statutes.

PROVISION OF LICENSING AGREEMENTS – Recognized educational, commercial, industrial, and governmental institutions and organizations, and others legitimately engaged in educational pursuits, including training, testing, and measurement activities, may address request for a licensing agreement to the copyright owners, who will determine whether, and under what conditions, including fees and charges, the materials in this book may be used them. In other words, a licensing facility exists for the legitimate use of the material in this book on other than an individual basis. However, it is asseverated and affirmed here that the material in this book CANNOT be used without the receipt of the express permission of such a licensing agreement from the Publishers. Inquiries re licensing should be addressed to the company, attention rights and permissions department.

All rights reserved, including the right of reproduction in whole or in part, in any form or by any means, electronic or mechanical, including photocopying, recording, or by any information storage and retrieval system, without permission in writing from the Publisher.

Copyright © 2024 by
National Learning Corporation

212 Michael Drive, Syosset, NY 11791
(516) 921-8888 • www.passbooks.com
E-mail: info@passbooks.com

PUBLISHED IN THE UNITED STATES OF AMERICA

PASSBOOK® SERIES

THE *PASSBOOK® SERIES* has been created to prepare applicants and candidates for the ultimate academic battlefield – the examination room.

At some time in our lives, each and every one of us may be required to take an examination – for validation, matriculation, admission, qualification, registration, certification, or licensure.

Based on the assumption that every applicant or candidate has met the basic formal educational standards, has taken the required number of courses, and read the necessary texts, the *PASSBOOK® SERIES* furnishes the one special preparation which may assure passing with confidence, instead of failing with insecurity. Examination questions – together with answers – are furnished as the basic vehicle for study so that the mysteries of the examination and its compounding difficulties may be eliminated or diminished by a sure method.

This book is meant to help you pass your examination provided that you qualify and are serious in your objective.

The entire field is reviewed through the huge store of content information which is succinctly presented through a provocative and challenging approach – the question-and-answer method.

A climate of success is established by furnishing the correct answers at the end of each test.

You soon learn to recognize types of questions, forms of questions, and patterns of questioning. You may even begin to anticipate expected outcomes.

You perceive that many questions are repeated or adapted so that you can gain acute insights, which may enable you to score many sure points.

You learn how to confront new questions, or types of questions, and to attack them confidently and work out the correct answers.

You note objectives and emphases, and recognize pitfalls and dangers, so that you may make positive educational adjustments.

Moreover, you are kept fully informed in relation to new concepts, methods, practices, and directions in the field.

You discover that you are actually taking the examination all the time: you are preparing for the examination by "taking" an examination, not by reading extraneous and/or supererogatory textbooks.

In short, this PASSBOOK®, used directedly, should be an important factor in helping you to pass your test.

POWER DISTRIBUTION MAINTAINER

DUTIES:

Power Distribution Maintainers, under supervision, maintain, install, inspect, test, alter and repair the direct current power distribution cable systems and contact rail systems in subways, elevated lines and yards. They install, maintain and inspect contact rail heaters, circuit breakers, third rail end approaches, wooden poles on the right of way, positive and negative cables, wires, relays and switches; inspect and replace insulators, protection boards and protection board brackets; bond negative rails; respond to emergencies and make emergency repairs; dig for and install ducts for cable installations; may perform welding and burning duties as required; drive a motor vehicle to and from work sites and load and unload vehicles as required; and perform related work.

SCOPE OF THE EXAMINATION:

The multiple-choice test may include questions on: the installation, maintenance and inspection of power distribution equipment; tools and electrical measuring devices used in power distribution work; electrical principles and theory; circuit schematics, electrical work including related computations; safe work practices and procedures; and other related areas.

HOW TO TAKE A TEST

I. YOU MUST PASS AN EXAMINATION

A. *WHAT EVERY CANDIDATE SHOULD KNOW*

Examination applicants often ask us for help in preparing for the written test. What can I study in advance? What kinds of questions will be asked? How will the test be given? How will the papers be graded?

As an applicant for a civil service examination, you may be wondering about some of these things. Our purpose here is to suggest effective methods of advance study and to describe civil service examinations.

Your chances for success on this examination can be increased if you know how to prepare. Those "pre-examination jitters" can be reduced if you know what to expect. You can even experience an adventure in good citizenship if you know why civil service exams are given.

B. *WHY ARE CIVIL SERVICE EXAMINATIONS GIVEN?*

Civil service examinations are important to you in two ways. As a citizen, you want public jobs filled by employees who know how to do their work. As a job seeker, you want a fair chance to compete for that job on an equal footing with other candidates. The best-known means of accomplishing this two-fold goal is the competitive examination.

Exams are widely publicized throughout the nation. They may be administered for jobs in federal, state, city, municipal, town or village governments or agencies.

Any citizen may apply, with some limitations, such as the age or residence of applicants. Your experience and education may be reviewed to see whether you meet the requirements for the particular examination. When these requirements exist, they are reasonable and applied consistently to all applicants. Thus, a competitive examination may cause you some uneasiness now, but it is your privilege and safeguard.

C. *HOW ARE CIVIL SERVICE EXAMS DEVELOPED?*

Examinations are carefully written by trained technicians who are specialists in the field known as "psychological measurement," in consultation with recognized authorities in the field of work that the test will cover. These experts recommend the subject matter areas or skills to be tested; only those knowledges or skills important to your success on the job are included. The most reliable books and source materials available are used as references. Together, the experts and technicians judge the difficulty level of the questions.

Test technicians know how to phrase questions so that the problem is clearly stated. Their ethics do not permit "trick" or "catch" questions. Questions may have been tried out on sample groups, or subjected to statistical analysis, to determine their usefulness.

Written tests are often used in combination with performance tests, ratings of training and experience, and oral interviews. All of these measures combine to form the best-known means of finding the right person for the right job.

II. HOW TO PASS THE WRITTEN TEST

A. NATURE OF THE EXAMINATION

To prepare intelligently for civil service examinations, you should know how they differ from school examinations you have taken. In school you were assigned certain definite pages to read or subjects to cover. The examination questions were quite detailed and usually emphasized memory. Civil service exams, on the other hand, try to discover your present ability to perform the duties of a position, plus your potentiality to learn these duties. In other words, a civil service exam attempts to predict how successful you will be. Questions cover such a broad area that they cannot be as minute and detailed as school exam questions.

In the public service similar kinds of work, or positions, are grouped together in one "class." This process is known as *position-classification*. All the positions in a class are paid according to the salary range for that class. One class title covers all of these positions, and they are all tested by the same examination.

B. FOUR BASIC STEPS

1) Study the announcement

How, then, can you know what subjects to study? Our best answer is: "Learn as much as possible about the class of positions for which you've applied." The exam will test the knowledge, skills and abilities needed to do the work.

Your most valuable source of information about the position you want is the official exam announcement. This announcement lists the training and experience qualifications. Check these standards and apply only if you come reasonably close to meeting them.

The brief description of the position in the examination announcement offers some clues to the subjects which will be tested. Think about the job itself. Review the duties in your mind. Can you perform them, or are there some in which you are rusty? Fill in the blank spots in your preparation.

Many jurisdictions preview the written test in the exam announcement by including a section called "Knowledge and Abilities Required," "Scope of the Examination," or some similar heading. Here you will find out specifically what fields will be tested.

2) Review your own background

Once you learn in general what the position is all about, and what you need to know to do the work, ask yourself which subjects you already know fairly well and which need improvement. You may wonder whether to concentrate on improving your strong areas or on building some background in your fields of weakness. When the announcement has specified "some knowledge" or "considerable knowledge," or has used adjectives like "beginning principles of…" or "advanced … methods," you can get a clue as to the number and difficulty of questions to be asked in any given field. More questions, and hence broader coverage, would be included for those subjects which are more important in the work. Now weigh your strengths and weaknesses against the job requirements and prepare accordingly.

3) Determine the level of the position

Another way to tell how intensively you should prepare is to understand the level of the job for which you are applying. Is it the entering level? In other words, is this the position in which beginners in a field of work are hired? Or is it an intermediate or advanced level? Sometimes this is indicated by such words as "Junior" or "Senior" in the class title. Other jurisdictions use Roman numerals to designate the level – Clerk I, Clerk II, for example. The word "Supervisor" sometimes appears in the title. If the level is not indicated by the title, check the description of duties. Will you be working under very close supervision, or will you have responsibility for independent decisions in this work?

4) Choose appropriate study materials

Now that you know the subjects to be examined and the relative amount of each subject to be covered, you can choose suitable study materials. For beginning level jobs, or even advanced ones, if you have a pronounced weakness in some aspect of your training, read a modern, standard textbook in that field. Be sure it is up to date and has general coverage. Such books are normally available at your library, and the librarian will be glad to help you locate one. For entry-level positions, questions of appropriate difficulty are chosen – neither highly advanced questions, nor those too simple. Such questions require careful thought but not advanced training.

If the position for which you are applying is technical or advanced, you will read more advanced, specialized material. If you are already familiar with the basic principles of your field, elementary textbooks would waste your time. Concentrate on advanced textbooks and technical periodicals. Think through the concepts and review difficult problems in your field.

These are all general sources. You can get more ideas on your own initiative, following these leads. For example, training manuals and publications of the government agency which employs workers in your field can be useful, particularly for technical and professional positions. A letter or visit to the government department involved may result in more specific study suggestions, and certainly will provide you with a more definite idea of the exact nature of the position you are seeking.

III. KINDS OF TESTS

Tests are used for purposes other than measuring knowledge and ability to perform specified duties. For some positions, it is equally important to test ability to make adjustments to new situations or to profit from training. In others, basic mental abilities not dependent on information are essential. Questions which test these things may not appear as pertinent to the duties of the position as those which test for knowledge and information. Yet they are often highly important parts of a fair examination. For very general questions, it is almost impossible to help you direct your study efforts. What we can do is to point out some of the more common of these general abilities needed in public service positions and describe some typical questions.

1) General information

Broad, general information has been found useful for predicting job success in some kinds of work. This is tested in a variety of ways, from vocabulary lists to questions about current events. Basic background in some field of work, such as sociology or economics, may be sampled in a group of questions. Often these are principles which have become familiar to most persons through exposure rather than through formal training. It is difficult to advise you how to study for these questions; being alert to the world around you is our best suggestion.

2) Verbal ability

An example of an ability needed in many positions is verbal or language ability. Verbal ability is, in brief, the ability to use and understand words. Vocabulary and grammar tests are typical measures of this ability. Reading comprehension or paragraph interpretation questions are common in many kinds of civil service tests. You are given a paragraph of written material and asked to find its central meaning.

3) Numerical ability

Number skills can be tested by the familiar arithmetic problem, by checking paired lists of numbers to see which are alike and which are different, or by interpreting charts and graphs. In the latter test, a graph may be printed in the test booklet which you are asked to use as the basis for answering questions.

4) Observation

A popular test for law-enforcement positions is the observation test. A picture is shown to you for several minutes, then taken away. Questions about the picture test your ability to observe both details and larger elements.

5) Following directions

In many positions in the public service, the employee must be able to carry out written instructions dependably and accurately. You may be given a chart with several columns, each column listing a variety of information. The questions require you to carry out directions involving the information given in the chart.

6) Skills and aptitudes

Performance tests effectively measure some manual skills and aptitudes. When the skill is one in which you are trained, such as typing or shorthand, you can practice. These tests are often very much like those given in business school or high school courses. For many of the other skills and aptitudes, however, no short-time preparation can be made. Skills and abilities natural to you or that you have developed throughout your lifetime are being tested.

Many of the general questions just described provide all the data needed to answer the questions and ask you to use your reasoning ability to find the answers. Your best preparation for these tests, as well as for tests of facts and ideas, is to be at your physical and mental best. You, no doubt, have your own methods of getting into an exam-taking mood and keeping "in shape." The next section lists some ideas on this subject.

IV. KINDS OF QUESTIONS

Only rarely is the "essay" question, which you answer in narrative form, used in civil service tests. Civil service tests are usually of the short-answer type. Full instructions for answering these questions will be given to you at the examination. But in case this is your first experience with short-answer questions and separate answer sheets, here is what you need to know:

1) Multiple-choice Questions

Most popular of the short-answer questions is the "multiple choice" or "best answer" question. It can be used, for example, to test for factual knowledge, ability to solve problems or judgment in meeting situations found at work.

A multiple-choice question is normally one of three types—
- It can begin with an incomplete statement followed by several possible endings. You are to find the one ending which *best* completes the statement, although some of the others may not be entirely wrong.
- It can also be a complete statement in the form of a question which is answered by choosing one of the statements listed.

- It can be in the form of a problem – again you select the best answer.

Here is an example of a multiple-choice question with a discussion which should give you some clues as to the method for choosing the right answer:

When an employee has a complaint about his assignment, the action which will *best* help him overcome his difficulty is to
- A. discuss his difficulty with his coworkers
- B. take the problem to the head of the organization
- C. take the problem to the person who gave him the assignment
- D. say nothing to anyone about his complaint

In answering this question, you should study each of the choices to find which is best. Consider choice "A" – Certainly an employee may discuss his complaint with fellow employees, but no change or improvement can result, and the complaint remains unresolved. Choice "B" is a poor choice since the head of the organization probably does not know what assignment you have been given, and taking your problem to him is known as "going over the head" of the supervisor. The supervisor, or person who made the assignment, is the person who can clarify it or correct any injustice. Choice "C" is, therefore, correct. To say nothing, as in choice "D," is unwise. Supervisors have and interest in knowing the problems employees are facing, and the employee is seeking a solution to his problem.

2) True/False Questions

The "true/false" or "right/wrong" form of question is sometimes used. Here a complete statement is given. Your job is to decide whether the statement is right or wrong.

SAMPLE: A roaming cell-phone call to a nearby city costs less than a non-roaming call to a distant city.

This statement is wrong, or false, since roaming calls are more expensive.

This is not a complete list of all possible question forms, although most of the others are variations of these common types. You will always get complete directions for answering questions. Be sure you understand *how* to mark your answers – ask questions until you do.

V. RECORDING YOUR ANSWERS

Computer terminals are used more and more today for many different kinds of exams.

For an examination with very few applicants, you may be told to record your answers in the test booklet itself. Separate answer sheets are much more common. If this separate answer sheet is to be scored by machine – and this is often the case – it is highly important that you mark your answers correctly in order to get credit.

An electronic scoring machine is often used in civil service offices because of the speed with which papers can be scored. Machine-scored answer sheets must be marked with a pencil, which will be given to you. This pencil has a high graphite content which responds to the electronic scoring machine. As a matter of fact, stray dots may register as answers, so do not let your pencil rest on the answer sheet while you are pondering the correct answer. Also, if your pencil lead breaks or is otherwise defective, ask for another.

Since the answer sheet will be dropped in a slot in the scoring machine, be careful not to bend the corners or get the paper crumpled.

The answer sheet normally has five vertical columns of numbers, with 30 numbers to a column. These numbers correspond to the question numbers in your test booklet. After each number, going across the page are four or five pairs of dotted lines. These short dotted lines have small letters or numbers above them. The first two pairs may also have a "T" or "F" above the letters. This indicates that the first two pairs only are to be used if the questions are of the true-false type. If the questions are multiple choice, disregard the "T" and "F" and pay attention only to the small letters or numbers.

Answer your questions in the manner of the sample that follows:

32. The largest city in the United States is
   A. Washington, D.C.
   B. New York City
   C. Chicago
   D. Detroit
   E. San Francisco

1) Choose the answer you think is best. (New York City is the largest, so "B" is correct.)
2) Find the row of dotted lines numbered the same as the question you are answering. (Find row number 32)
3) Find the pair of dotted lines corresponding to the answer. (Find the pair of lines under the mark "B.")
4) Make a solid black mark between the dotted lines.

VI. BEFORE THE TEST

Common sense will help you find procedures to follow to get ready for an examination. Too many of us, however, overlook these sensible measures. Indeed, nervousness and fatigue have been found to be the most serious reasons why applicants fail to do their best on civil service tests. Here is a list of reminders:

- Begin your preparation early – Don't wait until the last minute to go scurrying around for books and materials or to find out what the position is all about.
- Prepare continuously – An hour a night for a week is better than an all-night cram session. This has been definitely established. What is more, a night a week for a month will return better dividends than crowding your study into a shorter period of time.
- Locate the place of the exam – You have been sent a notice telling you when and where to report for the examination. If the location is in a different town or otherwise unfamiliar to you, it would be well to inquire the best route and learn something about the building.
- Relax the night before the test – Allow your mind to rest. Do not study at all that night. Plan some mild recreation or diversion; then go to bed early and get a good night's sleep.
- Get up early enough to make a leisurely trip to the place for the test – This way unforeseen events, traffic snarls, unfamiliar buildings, etc. will not upset you.
- Dress comfortably – A written test is not a fashion show. You will be known by number and not by name, so wear something comfortable.

- Leave excess paraphernalia at home – Shopping bags and odd bundles will get in your way. You need bring only the items mentioned in the official notice you received; usually everything you need is provided. Do not bring reference books to the exam. They will only confuse those last minutes and be taken away from you when in the test room.
- Arrive somewhat ahead of time – If because of transportation schedules you must get there very early, bring a newspaper or magazine to take your mind off yourself while waiting.
- Locate the examination room – When you have found the proper room, you will be directed to the seat or part of the room where you will sit. Sometimes you are given a sheet of instructions to read while you are waiting. Do not fill out any forms until you are told to do so; just read them and be prepared.
- Relax and prepare to listen to the instructions
- If you have any physical problem that may keep you from doing your best, be sure to tell the test administrator. If you are sick or in poor health, you really cannot do your best on the exam. You can come back and take the test some other time.

VII. AT THE TEST

The day of the test is here and you have the test booklet in your hand. The temptation to get going is very strong. Caution! There is more to success than knowing the right answers. You must know how to identify your papers and understand variations in the type of short-answer question used in this particular examination. Follow these suggestions for maximum results from your efforts:

1) Cooperate with the monitor

The test administrator has a duty to create a situation in which you can be as much at ease as possible. He will give instructions, tell you when to begin, check to see that you are marking your answer sheet correctly, and so on. He is not there to guard you, although he will see that your competitors do not take unfair advantage. He wants to help you do your best.

2) Listen to all instructions

Don't jump the gun! Wait until you understand all directions. In most civil service tests you get more time than you need to answer the questions. So don't be in a hurry. Read each word of instructions until you clearly understand the meaning. Study the examples, listen to all announcements and follow directions. Ask questions if you do not understand what to do.

3) Identify your papers

Civil service exams are usually identified by number only. You will be assigned a number; you must not put your name on your test papers. Be sure to copy your number correctly. Since more than one exam may be given, copy your exact examination title.

4) Plan your time

Unless you are told that a test is a "speed" or "rate of work" test, speed itself is usually not important. Time enough to answer all the questions will be provided, but this does not mean that you have all day. An overall time limit has been set. Divide the total time (in minutes) by the number of questions to determine the approximate time you have for each question.

5) Do not linger over difficult questions

If you come across a difficult question, mark it with a paper clip (useful to have along) and come back to it when you have been through the booklet. One caution if you do this – be sure to skip a number on your answer sheet as well. Check often to be sure that you have not lost your place and that you are marking in the row numbered the same as the question you are answering.

6) Read the questions

Be sure you know what the question asks! Many capable people are unsuccessful because they failed to *read* the questions correctly.

7) Answer all questions

Unless you have been instructed that a penalty will be deducted for incorrect answers, it is better to guess than to omit a question.

8) Speed tests

It is often better NOT to guess on speed tests. It has been found that on timed tests people are tempted to spend the last few seconds before time is called in marking answers at random – without even reading them – in the hope of picking up a few extra points. To discourage this practice, the instructions may warn you that your score will be "corrected" for guessing. That is, a penalty will be applied. The incorrect answers will be deducted from the correct ones, or some other penalty formula will be used.

9) Review your answers

If you finish before time is called, go back to the questions you guessed or omitted to give them further thought. Review other answers if you have time.

10) Return your test materials

If you are ready to leave before others have finished or time is called, take ALL your materials to the monitor and leave quietly. Never take any test material with you. The monitor can discover whose papers are not complete, and taking a test booklet may be grounds for disqualification.

VIII. EXAMINATION TECHNIQUES

1) Read the general instructions carefully. These are usually printed on the first page of the exam booklet. As a rule, these instructions refer to the timing of the examination; the fact that you should not start work until the signal and must stop work at a signal, etc. If there are any *special* instructions, such as a choice of questions to be answered, make sure that you note this instruction carefully.

2) When you are ready to start work on the examination, that is as soon as the signal has been given, read the instructions to each question booklet, underline any key words or phrases, such as *least, best, outline, describe* and the like. In this way you will tend to answer as requested rather than discover on reviewing your paper that you *listed without describing*, that you selected the *worst* choice rather than the *best* choice, etc.

3) If the examination is of the objective or multiple-choice type – that is, each question will also give a series of possible answers: A, B, C or D, and you are called upon to select the best answer and write the letter next to that answer on your answer paper – it is advisable to start answering each question in turn. There may be anywhere from 50 to 100 such questions in the three or four hours allotted and you can see how much time would be taken if you read through all the questions before beginning to answer any. Furthermore, if you come across a question or group of questions which you know would be difficult to answer, it would undoubtedly affect your handling of all the other questions.

4) If the examination is of the essay type and contains but a few questions, it is a moot point as to whether you should read all the questions before starting to answer any one. Of course, if you are given a choice – say five out of seven and the like – then it is essential to read all the questions so you can eliminate the two that are most difficult. If, however, you are asked to answer all the questions, there may be danger in trying to answer the easiest one first because you may find that you will spend too much time on it. The best technique is to answer the first question, then proceed to the second, etc.

5) Time your answers. Before the exam begins, write down the time it started, then add the time allowed for the examination and write down the time it must be completed, then divide the time available somewhat as follows:
    - If 3-1/2 hours are allowed, that would be 210 minutes. If you have 80 objective-type questions, that would be an average of 2-1/2 minutes per question. Allow yourself no more than 2 minutes per question, or a total of 160 minutes, which will permit about 50 minutes to review.
    - If for the time allotment of 210 minutes there are 7 essay questions to answer, that would average about 30 minutes a question. Give yourself only 25 minutes per question so that you have about 35 minutes to review.

6) The most important instruction is to *read each question* and make sure you know what is wanted. The second most important instruction is to *time yourself properly* so that you answer every question. The third most important instruction is to *answer every question*. Guess if you have to but include something for each question. Remember that you will receive no credit for a blank and will probably receive some credit if you write something in answer to an essay question. If you guess a letter – say "B" for a multiple-choice question – you may have guessed right. If you leave a blank as an answer to a multiple-choice question, the examiners may respect your feelings but it will not add a point to your score. Some exams may penalize you for wrong answers, so in such cases *only*, you may not want to guess unless you have some basis for your answer.

7) Suggestions
    a. Objective-type questions
        1. Examine the question booklet for proper sequence of pages and questions
        2. Read all instructions carefully
        3. Skip any question which seems too difficult; return to it after all other questions have been answered
        4. Apportion your time properly; do not spend too much time on any single question or group of questions

5. Note and underline key words – *all, most, fewest, least, best, worst, same, opposite,* etc.
6. Pay particular attention to negatives
7. Note unusual option, e.g., unduly long, short, complex, different or similar in content to the body of the question
8. Observe the use of "hedging" words – *probably, may, most likely,* etc.
9. Make sure that your answer is put next to the same number as the question
10. Do not second-guess unless you have good reason to believe the second answer is definitely more correct
11. Cross out original answer if you decide another answer is more accurate; do not erase until you are ready to hand your paper in
12. Answer all questions; guess unless instructed otherwise
13. Leave time for review

    b. Essay questions
      1. Read each question carefully
      2. Determine exactly what is wanted. Underline key words or phrases.
      3. Decide on outline or paragraph answer
      4. Include many different points and elements unless asked to develop any one or two points or elements
      5. Show impartiality by giving pros and cons unless directed to select one side only
      6. Make and write down any assumptions you find necessary to answer the questions
      7. Watch your English, grammar, punctuation and choice of words
      8. Time your answers; don't crowd material

8) Answering the essay question

Most essay questions can be answered by framing the specific response around several key words or ideas. Here are a few such key words or ideas:

M's: manpower, materials, methods, money, management
P's: purpose, program, policy, plan, procedure, practice, problems, pitfalls, personnel, public relations

    a. Six basic steps in handling problems:
      1. Preliminary plan and background development
      2. Collect information, data and facts
      3. Analyze and interpret information, data and facts
      4. Analyze and develop solutions as well as make recommendations
      5. Prepare report and sell recommendations
      6. Install recommendations and follow up effectiveness

    b. Pitfalls to avoid
      1. *Taking things for granted* – A statement of the situation does not necessarily imply that each of the elements is necessarily true; for example, a complaint may be invalid and biased so that all that can be taken for granted is that a complaint has been registered

2. *Considering only one side of a situation* – Wherever possible, indicate several alternatives and then point out the reasons you selected the best one
3. *Failing to indicate follow up* – Whenever your answer indicates action on your part, make certain that you will take proper follow-up action to see how successful your recommendations, procedures or actions turn out to be
4. *Taking too long in answering any single question* – Remember to time your answers properly

IX. AFTER THE TEST

Scoring procedures differ in detail among civil service jurisdictions although the general principles are the same. Whether the papers are hand-scored or graded by machine we have described, they are nearly always graded by number. That is, the person who marks the paper knows only the number – never the name – of the applicant. Not until all the papers have been graded will they be matched with names. If other tests, such as training and experience or oral interview ratings have been given, scores will be combined. Different parts of the examination usually have different weights. For example, the written test might count 60 percent of the final grade, and a rating of training and experience 40 percent. In many jurisdictions, veterans will have a certain number of points added to their grades.

After the final grade has been determined, the names are placed in grade order and an eligible list is established. There are various methods for resolving ties between those who get the same final grade – probably the most common is to place first the name of the person whose application was received first. Job offers are made from the eligible list in the order the names appear on it. You will be notified of your grade and your rank as soon as all these computations have been made. This will be done as rapidly as possible.

People who are found to meet the requirements in the announcement are called "eligibles." Their names are put on a list of eligible candidates. An eligible's chances of getting a job depend on how high he stands on this list and how fast agencies are filling jobs from the list.

When a job is to be filled from a list of eligibles, the agency asks for the names of people on the list of eligibles for that job. When the civil service commission receives this request, it sends to the agency the names of the three people highest on this list. Or, if the job to be filled has specialized requirements, the office sends the agency the names of the top three persons who meet these requirements from the general list.

The appointing officer makes a choice from among the three people whose names were sent to him. If the selected person accepts the appointment, the names of the others are put back on the list to be considered for future openings.

That is the rule in hiring from all kinds of eligible lists, whether they are for typist, carpenter, chemist, or something else. For every vacancy, the appointing officer has his choice of any one of the top three eligibles on the list. This explains why the person whose name is on top of the list sometimes does not get an appointment when some of the persons lower on the list do. If the appointing officer chooses the second or third eligible, the No. 1 eligible does not get a job at once, but stays on the list until he is appointed or the list is terminated.

X. HOW TO PASS THE INTERVIEW TEST

The examination for which you applied requires an oral interview test. You have already taken the written test and you are now being called for the interview test – the final part of the formal examination.

You may think that it is not possible to prepare for an interview test and that there are no procedures to follow during an interview. Our purpose is to point out some things you can do in advance that will help you and some good rules to follow and pitfalls to avoid while you are being interviewed.

What is an interview supposed to test?

The written examination is designed to test the technical knowledge and competence of the candidate; the oral is designed to evaluate intangible qualities, not readily measured otherwise, and to establish a list showing the relative fitness of each candidate – as measured against his competitors – for the position sought. Scoring is not on the basis of "right" and "wrong," but on a sliding scale of values ranging from "not passable" to "outstanding." As a matter of fact, it is possible to achieve a relatively low score without a single "incorrect" answer because of evident weakness in the qualities being measured.

Occasionally, an examination may consist entirely of an oral test – either an individual or a group oral. In such cases, information is sought concerning the technical knowledges and abilities of the candidate, since there has been no written examination for this purpose. More commonly, however, an oral test is used to supplement a written examination.

Who conducts interviews?

The composition of oral boards varies among different jurisdictions. In nearly all, a representative of the personnel department serves as chairman. One of the members of the board may be a representative of the department in which the candidate would work. In some cases, "outside experts" are used, and, frequently, a businessman or some other representative of the general public is asked to serve. Labor and management or other special groups may be represented. The aim is to secure the services of experts in the appropriate field.

However the board is composed, it is a good idea (and not at all improper or unethical) to ascertain in advance of the interview who the members are and what groups they represent. When you are introduced to them, you will have some idea of their backgrounds and interests, and at least you will not stutter and stammer over their names.

What should be done before the interview?

While knowledge about the board members is useful and takes some of the surprise element out of the interview, there is other preparation which is more substantive. It *is* possible to prepare for an oral interview – in several ways:

1) Keep a copy of your application and review it carefully before the interview

This may be the only document before the oral board, and the starting point of the interview. Know what education and experience you have listed there, and the sequence and dates of all of it. Sometimes the board will ask you to review the highlights of your experience for them; you should not have to hem and haw doing it.

2) Study the class specification and the examination announcement

Usually, the oral board has one or both of these to guide them. The qualities, characteristics or knowledges required by the position sought are stated in these documents. They offer valuable clues as to the nature of the oral interview. For example, if the job involves supervisory responsibilities, the announcement will usually indicate that knowledge of modern supervisory methods and the qualifications of the candidate as a supervisor will be tested. If so, you can expect such questions, frequently in the form of a hypothetical situation which you are expected to solve. NEVER go into an oral without knowledge of the duties and responsibilities of the job you seek.

3) Think through each qualification required

Try to visualize the kind of questions you would ask if you were a board member. How well could you answer them? Try especially to appraise your own knowledge and background in each area, *measured against the job sought*, and identify any areas in which you are weak. Be critical and realistic – do not flatter yourself.

4) Do some general reading in areas in which you feel you may be weak

For example, if the job involves supervision and your past experience has NOT, some general reading in supervisory methods and practices, particularly in the field of human relations, might be useful. Do NOT study agency procedures or detailed manuals. The oral board will be testing your understanding and capacity, not your memory.

5) Get a good night's sleep and watch your general health and mental attitude

You will want a clear head at the interview. Take care of a cold or any other minor ailment, and of course, no hangovers.

What should be done on the day of the interview?

Now comes the day of the interview itself. Give yourself plenty of time to get there. Plan to arrive somewhat ahead of the scheduled time, particularly if your appointment is in the fore part of the day. If a previous candidate fails to appear, the board might be ready for you a bit early. By early afternoon an oral board is almost invariably behind schedule if there are many candidates, and you may have to wait. Take along a book or magazine to read, or your application to review, but leave any extraneous material in the waiting room when you go in for your interview. In any event, relax and compose yourself.

The matter of dress is important. The board is forming impressions about you – from your experience, your manners, your attitude, and your appearance. Give your personal appearance careful attention. Dress your best, but not your flashiest. Choose conservative, appropriate clothing, and be sure it is immaculate. This is a business interview, and your appearance should indicate that you regard it as such. Besides, being well groomed and properly dressed will help boost your confidence.

Sooner or later, someone will call your name and escort you into the interview room. *This is it.* From here on you are on your own. It is too late for any more preparation. But remember, you asked for this opportunity to prove your fitness, and you are here because your request was granted.

What happens when you go in?

The usual sequence of events will be as follows: The clerk (who is often the board stenographer) will introduce you to the chairman of the oral board, who will introduce you to the other members of the board. Acknowledge the introductions before you sit down. Do not be surprised if you find a microphone facing you or a stenotypist sitting by. Oral interviews are usually recorded in the event of an appeal or other review.

Usually the chairman of the board will open the interview by reviewing the highlights of your education and work experience from your application – primarily for the benefit of the other members of the board, as well as to get the material into the record. Do not interrupt or comment unless there is an error or significant misinterpretation; if that is the case, do not hesitate. But do not quibble about insignificant matters. Also, he will usually ask you some question about your education, experience or your present job – partly to get you to start talking and to establish the interviewing "rapport." He may start the actual questioning, or turn it over to one of the other members. Frequently, each member undertakes the questioning on a particular area, one in which he is perhaps most competent, so you can expect each member to participate in the examination. Because time is limited, you may also expect some rather abrupt switches in the direction the questioning takes, so do not be upset by it. Normally, a board member will not pursue a single line of questioning unless he discovers a particular strength or weakness.

After each member has participated, the chairman will usually ask whether any member has any further questions, then will ask you if you have anything you wish to add. Unless you are expecting this question, it may floor you. Worse, it may start you off on an extended, extemporaneous speech. The board is not usually seeking more information. The question is principally to offer you a last opportunity to present further qualifications or to indicate that you have nothing to add. So, if you feel that a significant qualification or characteristic has been overlooked, it is proper to point it out in a sentence or so. Do not compliment the board on the thoroughness of their examination – they have been sketchy, and you know it. If you wish, merely say, "No thank you, I have nothing further to add." This is a point where you can "talk yourself out" of a good impression or fail to present an important bit of information. Remember, *you close the interview yourself*.

The chairman will then say, "That is all, Mr. _____, thank you." Do not be startled; the interview is over, and quicker than you think. Thank him, gather your belongings and take your leave. Save your sigh of relief for the other side of the door.

How to put your best foot forward

Throughout this entire process, you may feel that the board individually and collectively is trying to pierce your defenses, seek out your hidden weaknesses and embarrass and confuse you. Actually, this is not true. They are obliged to make an appraisal of your qualifications for the job you are seeking, and they want to see you in your best light. Remember, they must interview all candidates and a non-cooperative candidate may become a failure in spite of their best efforts to bring out his qualifications. Here are 15 suggestions that will help you:

1) Be natural – Keep your attitude confident, not cocky

If you are not confident that you can do the job, do not expect the board to be. Do not apologize for your weaknesses, try to bring out your strong points. The board is interested in a positive, not negative, presentation. Cockiness will antagonize any board member and make him wonder if you are covering up a weakness by a false show of strength.

2) Get comfortable, but don't lounge or sprawl

Sit erectly but not stiffly. A careless posture may lead the board to conclude that you are careless in other things, or at least that you are not impressed by the importance of the occasion. Either conclusion is natural, even if incorrect. Do not fuss with your clothing, a pencil or an ashtray. Your hands may occasionally be useful to emphasize a point; do not let them become a point of distraction.

3) Do not wisecrack or make small talk

This is a serious situation, and your attitude should show that you consider it as such. Further, the time of the board is limited – they do not want to waste it, and neither should you.

4) Do not exaggerate your experience or abilities

In the first place, from information in the application or other interviews and sources, the board may know more about you than you think. Secondly, you probably will not get away with it. An experienced board is rather adept at spotting such a situation, so do not take the chance.

5) If you know a board member, do not make a point of it, yet do not hide it

Certainly you are not fooling him, and probably not the other members of the board. Do not try to take advantage of your acquaintanceship – it will probably do you little good.

6) Do not dominate the interview

Let the board do that. They will give you the clues – do not assume that you have to do all the talking. Realize that the board has a number of questions to ask you, and do not try to take up all the interview time by showing off your extensive knowledge of the answer to the first one.

7) Be attentive

You only have 20 minutes or so, and you should keep your attention at its sharpest throughout. When a member is addressing a problem or question to you, give him your undivided attention. Address your reply principally to him, but do not exclude the other board members.

8) Do not interrupt

A board member may be stating a problem for you to analyze. He will ask you a question when the time comes. Let him state the problem, and wait for the question.

9) Make sure you understand the question

Do not try to answer until you are sure what the question is. If it is not clear, restate it in your own words or ask the board member to clarify it for you. However, do not haggle about minor elements.

10) Reply promptly but not hastily

A common entry on oral board rating sheets is "candidate responded readily," or "candidate hesitated in replies." Respond as promptly and quickly as you can, but do not jump to a hasty, ill-considered answer.

11) Do not be peremptory in your answers

A brief answer is proper – but do not fire your answer back. That is a losing game from your point of view. The board member can probably ask questions much faster than you can answer them.

12) Do not try to create the answer you think the board member wants

He is interested in what kind of mind you have and how it works – not in playing games. Furthermore, he can usually spot this practice and will actually grade you down on it.

13) Do not switch sides in your reply merely to agree with a board member

Frequently, a member will take a contrary position merely to draw you out and to see if you are willing and able to defend your point of view. Do not start a debate, yet do not surrender a good position. If a position is worth taking, it is worth defending.

14) Do not be afraid to admit an error in judgment if you are shown to be wrong

The board knows that you are forced to reply without any opportunity for careful consideration. Your answer may be demonstrably wrong. If so, admit it and get on with the interview.

15) Do not dwell at length on your present job

The opening question may relate to your present assignment. Answer the question but do not go into an extended discussion. You are being examined for a *new* job, not your present one. As a matter of fact, try to phrase ALL your answers in terms of the job for which you are being examined.

Basis of Rating

Probably you will forget most of these "do's" and "don'ts" when you walk into the oral interview room. Even remembering them all will not ensure you a passing grade. Perhaps you did not have the qualifications in the first place. But remembering them will help you to put your best foot forward, without treading on the toes of the board members.

Rumor and popular opinion to the contrary notwithstanding, an oral board wants you to make the best appearance possible. They know you are under pressure – but they also want to see how you respond to it as a guide to what your reaction would be under the pressures of the job you seek. They will be influenced by the degree of poise you display, the personal traits you show and the manner in which you respond.

ABOUT THIS BOOK

This book contains tests divided into Examination Sections. Go through each test, answering every question in the margin. We have also attached a sample answer sheet at the back of the book that can be removed and used. At the end of each test look at the answer key and check your answers. On the ones you got wrong, look at the right answer choice and learn. Do not fill in the answers first. Do not memorize the questions and answers, but understand the answer and principles involved. On your test, the questions will likely be different from the samples. Questions are changed and new ones added. If you understand these past questions you should have success with any changes that arise. Tests may consist of several types of questions. We have additional books on each subject should more study be advisable or necessary for you. Finally, the more you study, the better prepared you will be. This book is intended to be the last thing you study before you walk into the examination room. Prior study of relevant texts is also recommended. NLC publishes some of these in our Fundamental Series. Knowledge and good sense are important factors in passing your exam. Good luck also helps. So now study this Passbook, absorb the material contained within and take that knowledge into the examination. Then do your best to pass that exam.

EXAMINATION SECTION

EXAMINATION SECTION
TEST 1

DIRECTIONS: Each question or incomplete statement is followed by several suggested answers or completions. Select the one that BEST answers the question or completes the statement. *PRINT THE LETTER OF THE CORRECT ANSWER IN THE SPACE AT THE RIGHT.*

1. The dielectric strength of the insulation of a cable is measured with a(n) 1.____

    A. voltmeter
    B. ammeter
    C. megger
    D. tension meter

2. A sharp-edged tool should not be carried in a maintainer's pocket PRIMARILY because the 2.____

    A. tool could be easily lost
    B. maintainer's helper may be looking for the tool
    C. tool may cut the maintainer's skin
    D. tool may be brought to the maintainer's clothes locker rather than the tool room

3. The gauge of the running rails is the _____ of the running rails. 3.____

    A. thickness
    B. height
    C. distance between the inside edges
    D. distance between the outside edges

4. When a fire is being hosed with a fire extinguisher, the discharge should be directed at the _____ the fire. 4.____

    A. highest flames of
    B. smoke from
    C. area in front of
    D. base of

5. In contact rail work, *anchors* are used to 5.____

    A. prevent the contact rail from moving lengthwise
    B. reduce vibrations in the contact rail
    C. support the contact rail protection board
    D. prevent the ties from cracking under the weight of the contact rail supports

6. A circuit breaker is considered *trip-free* if 6.____

    A. it is not latched in position when closed
    B. the closing and tripping operations are independent of each other
    C. the tripping devices operate easily
    D. it cannot be tripped

7. When may a maintainer who is on transit property play cards? 7.____

    A. Only during the lunch period
    B. At no time
    C. When he is not busy
    D. When his foreman is not present

8. A slight coating of rust on a screwdriver is BEST removed by _____ the screwdriver with _____.

   A. scraping; a knife
   B. rubbing; a damp cloth
   C. rubbing; kerosene and fine steel wool
   D. rubbing; fine sandpaper

9. Contact rail weights are USUALLY given in pounds per

   A. inch
   B. foot
   C. yard
   D. cubic foot

10. The MAIN purpose of carbon contacts in an air circuit breaker is to

    A. *protect* the main contacts against arcing
    B. *protect* the main contacts against overheating
    C. *isolate* the circuit breaker during maintenance
    D. *protect* the main contacts against rusting

Questions 11-18.

DIRECTIONS: Questions 11 through 18 refer to the circuit diagram shown below, which consists of resistors and one-relay coil resistance.

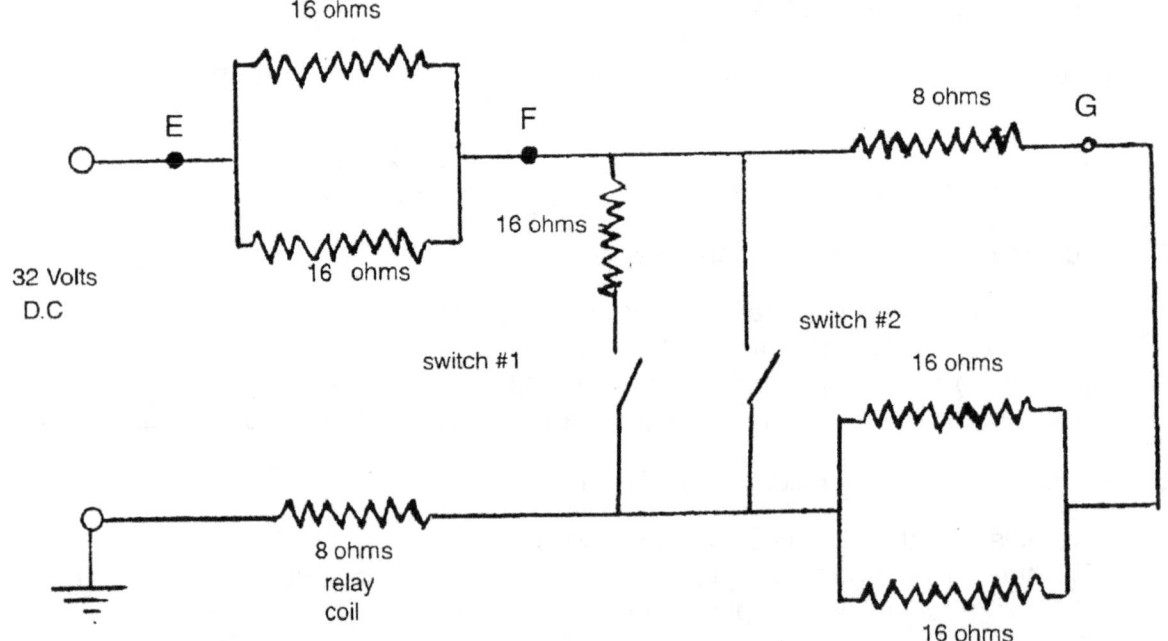

11. If both switches #1 and #2 are open, the current at point G is _____ ampere(s).

    A. 0.4   B. 0.8   C. 1   D. 2

12. If both switches #1 and #2 are open, the voltage drop from point E to point F is _____ volt(s).

    A. 0.5   B. 1   C. 8   D. 16

13. If switch #2 is closed, the current at point F is _____ ampere(s). 13.____
    A. 0.8 B. 1.6 C. 1 D. 2

14. If both switches #1 and #2 are closed, the current at point F is _____ ampere(s). 14.____
    A. 0.4 B. 0.8 C. 1 D. 2

15. If switch #1 is closed and switch #2 is open, the current at point F is _____ ampere(s). 15.____
    A. 2/3 B. 1 C. 1 1/3 D. 2 2/3

16. If both switches #1 and #2 are open, the power dissipated in the 8-ohm relay coil resistance is _____ watts. 16.____
    A. 2 B. 4 C. 8 D. 16

17. If both switches #1 and #2 are open and a ground develops at point G, the current flowing through the 8-ohm resistor is _____ ampere(s). 17.____
    A. 1/2 B. 1 C. 1 1/2 D. 2

18. If both switches #1 and #2 are closed, what value of resistance should replace the 8-ohm relay coil resistance so that the current at point F is 1/2 ampere? _____ ohms. 18.____
    A. 56 B. 64 C. 72 D. 80

19. Jumper cable connections to the contact rail should be installed 19.____
    A. *without* slack to avoid a tripping hazard
    B. *without* slack to save material
    C. *with* slack to avoid tension in the cable
    D. *with* slack so that the jumper end can be relocated later if necessary

20. Welded negative rail bonds are USUALLY attached to the _____ side of the rail _____. 20.____
    A. *inner;* head   B. *inner;* web
    C. *outer;* head   D. *outer;* web

KEY (CORRECT ANSWERS)

1.	C	11.	C
2.	C	12.	C
3.	C	13.	D
4.	D	14.	D
5.	A	15.	C
6.	B	16.	C
7.	B	17.	D
8.	C	18.	A
9.	C	19.	C
10.	A	20.	C

TEST 2

DIRECTIONS: Each question or incomplete statement is followed by several suggested answers or completions. Select the one that BEST answers the question or completes the statement. *PRINT THE LETTER OF THE CORRECT ANSWER IN THE SPACE AT THE RIGHT.*

1. Which of the following statements is TRUE about the use of an electric power drill which operates on third rail power?
   The _____ lead should be _____.

   A. *negative;* connected to the signal rail
   B. *negative;* connected to the third rail
   C. *positive;* connected before the negative lead
   D. *positive;* disconnected before the negative lead

2. Electric power is measured with a(n)

   A. ammeter   B. voltmeter
   C. wattmeter   D. megger

3. A lag screw is easily removed from a protection board with a _____ wrench.

   A. Stillson   B. pin   C. box   D. strap

4. For bare copper wire of equal lengths, the No. 12 gauge wire, when compared to the No. 18 gauge wire, has

   A. less weight   B. more conductivity
   C. more resistance   D. less cross-sectional area

5. Forty boxes of bolts weigh 1,000 pounds. Each empty box weighs four pounds. The weight of the bolts in each box is _____ pounds.

   A. 17   B. 21   C. 25   D. 29

6. When grinding a weld smooth, it is MOST important to avoid

   A. grinding too slowly
   B. overheating the grinding wheel
   C. grinding too much of the weld away
   D. grinding after the weld has cooled off

7. Blowout coils on circuit breakers are used to

   A. help extinguish the arc when the circuit is opened
   B. help extinguish the arc when the circuit is closed
   C. open the circuit breaker when there is a short circuit
   D. sound an alarm when there is a short circuit

8. A size of a positive feeder cable used by the power distribution section is

   A. 600 c.m.   B. 2,000,000 c.m.
   C. No. 12 A.W.G.   D. No. 2 A.W.G.

9. Metal conduit is galvanized to

   A. add mechanical strength to the metal
   B. make the conduit into a good insulator
   C. prevent the conduit from corroding
   D. make it easier to bend

10. Of the following, the condition that is the MOST serious is a

    A. broken negative rail bond
    B. leak on a signal air line
    C. broken automatic stop trip arm
    D. broken running rail

11. A stationing of 103 + 50 means

    A. 103.50 feet
    B. 103 feet north and 50 feet east
    C. 103 yards and 50 feet
    D. 10,350 feet

12. Rigid metal conduit should be reamed after cutting to

    A. remove burrs from the conduit
    B. make the edge of the conduit dull
    C. clear out the rust
    D. remove dents from the end of the conduit

13. If a drawing has a scale of 1/4" =1', a dimension of 1 3/4" on the drawing would be equal to

    A. 4'   B. 5'   C. 6'   D. 7'

14. A certain negative rail joint has two rail bonds. If one of the rail bonds should break off, the MOST likely result is that the

    A. remaining bond would fail at once due to overcurrent
    B. track circuit breaker would trip
    C. circuit would keep functioning but the remaining bond would get hotter
    D. trains would have to travel slower

15. The EASIEST way to determine whether a contact rail is alive is to use a(n)

    A. bank of lights   B. voltmeter
    C. wattmeter   D. ohmmeter

16. The device or material that is used to remove moisture from a Cadweld machine is a(n)

    A. 75% solution of alcohol and water
    B. 50-50 solution of alcohol and water
    C. oxyacetylene torch
    D. propane torch

17. The centering cup that locates the insulator for the contact rail is secured to the ties with a

   A. steel-through-bolt B. galvanized lag screw
   C. steel spike D. wooden dowel

18. The holes in contact rails are made by

   A. burning B. drilling C. punching D. grinding

19. A wood screw which can be tightened with a wrench is known as a _____ screw.

   A. Phillips B. Dardelet C. lag D. jack

20. The cleats for supporting power cables are USUALLY made of

   A. steel B. porcelain C. rubber D. wood

KEY (CORRECT ANSWERS)

1.	D	11.	D
2.	C	12.	A
3.	C	13.	D
4.	B	14.	C
5.	B	15.	A
6.	C	16.	D
7.	A	17.	B
8.	B	18.	B
9.	C	19.	C
10.	D	20.	D

EXAMINATION SECTION
TEST 1

DIRECTIONS: Each question or incomplete statement is followed by several suggested answers or completions. Select the one that BEST answers the question or completes the statement. *PRINT THE LETTER OF THE CORRECT ANSWER IN THE SPACE AT THE RIGHT.*

1. When contact rails are installed, brackets are required for the 1.____
    A. contact rail insulators
    B. protection board
    C. contact rail ties
    D. anchors

2. The fuse in a certain circuit has blown and is replaced by the maintainer with a fuse of the same rating, which also blows when the switch is closed. The maintainer should FIRST 2.____
    A. replace the fuse with one of a higher voltage rating
    B. replace the fuse with one of a higher current rating
    C. check the circuit
    D. replace the fuse with a heavy piece of copper wire

3. Of the following statements concerning track rail bonds and contact rail jumpers, which one is CORRECT? 3.____
    A. Contact rail jumpers are insulated while track rail bonds are not insulated.
    B. Track rail bonds are insulated while contact rail jumpers are not insulated.
    C. Both contact rail jumpers and track rail bonds are insulated.
    D. Contact rail jumpers and track rail bonds are not insulated.

4. When a D.C. circuit is to be opened with a standard knife switch, it should be opened 4.____
    A. *slowly,* to prevent an instantaneous high voltage
    B. *slowly,* to avoid mechanical damage to the switch
    C. *rapidly,* to avoid blowing the fuse
    D. *rapidly,* to extinguish the arc quickly

5. A contact rail insulator should be replaced if it is 5.____
    A. old
    B. damp
    C. discolored
    D. chipped

6. On a section of a four-track road, operation of the emergency alarm box will usually remove the power on 6.____
    A. only one track
    B. only two of the tracks
    C. all four of the tracks
    D. only the tracks that are adjacent to the alarm box

7. When a fuse clip becomes hot under normal load, of the following, the MOST likely reason is that the 7.____
    A. rating of the fuse is too high
    B. rating of the fuse is too low

C. contact between the fuse and the clip is poor
D. clip is under too much tension

8. The abbreviation S.P.S.T. is used to describe a certain type of

   A. wire B. cable
   C. switch D. circuit breaker

9. A blue light indicates the location of an emergency alarm box, a telephone, and a(n)

   A. ladder B. emergency exit
   C. first aid kit D. fire extinguisher

10. Heavy copper bonds at track rail joints indicate that this rail is carrying the _____ current.

    A. signal rail B. tunnel lighting
    C. negative return D. A.C.

11. When a maintainer opens a switch in a certain circuit on which he is going to work, the procedure he should follow to make certain that no one restores power to the circuit is to

    A. block the switch open and place a hold-off tag on the switch
    B. ground both terminals of the switch
    C. verbally inform other maintainers who are working in the vicinity that work is being done on the circuit controlled by that switch
    D. keep a helper stationed at the switch

12. Rubber mats are provided on the floor of circuit breaker houses both in front and in back of the panel boards as a precaution against the possibility of

    A. an employee slipping
    B. an employee receiving an electric shock
    C. the floor getting too hot
    D. the floor wearing because of heavy traffic

13. A lamp bank has been connected to the contact rail along the right of way, but it does not light. Of the following, the BEST method of determining whether this lamp bank is defective is to

    A. test each lamp individually with a voltmeter
    B. test each socket shell to ground with an ammeter
    C. test the circuit fuse at the circuit breaker
    D. observe whether a known good lamp bank lights when connected to the same circuit

14. The end of the protection board is required to overhang an end approach by

    A. 3" B. 4" C. 5" D. 6"

15. A circular mil is a unit of

    A. length B. area C. volume D. weight

16. One advantage of rubber insulation is that it

A. is not damaged by oil
B. is able to withstand high temperatures
C. is fireproof
D. does not absorb much moisture

17. Rubber gloves should be given a final check for pinholes by the

   A. person issuing them from the stock room
   B. foreman in charge of the work gang
   C. safety unit
   D. man about to use them

18. The material for contact rail insulators should be

   A. rubber   B. PVC   C. porcelain   D. wood

19. To raise or lower one end of a contact rail in order to place the rail in its proper position, a maintainer should use a

   A. bronze pry bar   B. wooden pry bar
   C. steel pry bar   D. steel pick

20. The gauge number of a bit for a drill refers to the _____ the bit.

   A. length of   B. hardness of
   C. diameter of   D. threads per inch on

KEY (CORRECT ANSWERS)

1.	B	11.	A
2.	C	12.	B
3.	A	13.	D
4.	D	14.	A
5.	D	15.	B
6.	C	16.	D
7.	C	17.	D
8.	C	18.	C
9.	D	19.	B
10.	C	20.	C

TEST 2

DIRECTIONS: Each question or incomplete statement is followed by several suggested answers or completions. Select the one that BEST answers the question or completes the statement. *PRINT THE LETTER OF THE CORRECT ANSWER IN THE SPACE AT THE RIGHT.*

1. Before a Cadweld joint can be made, the surface of the contact rail must be   1.____

   A. tinned
   B. ground bright and shiny
   C. chamfered
   D. roughened

2. When a contact rail does NOT rest properly on an insulator, shims may be inserted between the   2.____

   A. cap and the insulator
   B. centering cup and the insulator
   C. cap and the contact rail
   D. protection board bracket and the insulator

3. The sum of the following dimensions, 2'7 1/4", 1'8 1/2", 2'1/16", and 3/4", is   3.____

   A. 5'15 9/16"
   B. 5'15 11/16"
   C. 5'7/16"
   D. 6'4 9/16"

4. If a 3-foot length of contact rail weighs 150 pounds, then 39 feet of contact rail weighs _____ pounds.   4.____

   A. 1850   B. 1900   C. 1950   D. 2000

5. A high spot-temperature on a bonded negative rail joint is generally due to   5.____

   A. an open circuit
   B. a short circuit
   C. excessive voltage applied to the contact rail
   D. a defective connection

Questions 6-10.

DIRECTIONS: Questions 6 through 10 refer to standard flagging instructions.

6. The green lamp should be displayed a specified minimum distance beyond the furthest point of work. This distance is   6.____

   A. 100 feet
   B. 500 feet
   C. 700 feet
   D. the length of the longest train

7. An acceptable distance for the yellow lamps to be displayed from the red lamp is _____ feet.   7.____

   A. 100   B. 300   C. 600   D. 900

8. The last lamp to be removed from its fixed position on the trackway is the _____ lamp.   8.____

A. green B. red C. white D. yellow

9. If train speeds on a particular track are to be temporarily reduced to no more than ten miles per hour without the stationing of a flagman, the number of yellow lamps that should be displayed on the track is

A. 1 B. 2 C. 3 D. 4

10. When a flagman protects a work gang, he should give the *proceed* signal to the motorman

A. as soon as the motorman gives two short blasts of his horn
B. when the motorman brings the train to a complete stop at the specified distance from the work gang
C. before the motorman brings the train to a complete stop
D. when the employee in charge of the work gang indicates that the man and the track are clear

11. The MINIMUM number of lamps required to properly protect a power distribution gang working along a single track is

A. 3 B. 4 C. 5 D. 6

12. A *No Clearance* area long the right-of-way should be indicated by a sign that

A. is yellow
B. is red
C. has diagonal black stripes on a white background
D. has diagonal red stripes on a white background

13. In a mercury arc rectifier, an increase in the number of phases causes _____ ripple in the output voltage.

A. decreased
B. increased
C. no change of the
D. the complete removal of

14. Of the following, the MOST desirable way to light an acetylene torch is with a

A. match B. friction igniter
C. gas-operated burner D. burning piece of paper

15. When a maintainer works on a circuit breaker, he should ALWAYS

A. disconnect the live feeder cable from the circuit breaker
B. assume that he is working with live circuits
C. make certain that the circuit breaker is completely de-energized
D. disconnect the equalizer bus from the circuit breaker

16. Contact rail-side approaches in many areas have been replaced with

A. dipped contact rail B. contact rail anchors
C. expansion joints D. anticreepers

17. After cables are pulled through underground ducts, the ends of the ducts should be thoroughly caulked with 17.____

   A. paraffin   B. insulatum   C. oakum   D. tar

18. A piece of safety equipment that is usually NOT needed when removing a feeder cable terminal from a circuit breaker stud is a(n) 18.____

   A. insulated wrench   B. rubber mat
   C. pair of goggles   D. pair of rubber gloves

19. Expansion joints in the contact rail are necessary to prevent 19.____

   A. movement of the contact rail
   B. buckling of the contact rail
   C. electrical shocks at contact rail joints
   D. damage to the contact rail insulators

20. A voltmeter will give the MOST accurate reading when the range selected is such that the pointer settles at the _____ of the scale. 20.____

   A. exact middle   B. upper end
   C. lower end   D. exact lower 1/3

KEY (CORRECT ANSWERS)

1.	B	11.	C
2.	A	12.	D
3.	D	13.	A
4.	C	14.	B
5.	D	15.	B
6.	D	16.	A
7.	C	17.	C
8.	A	18.	C
9.	C	19.	B
10.	D	20.	B

EXAMINATION SECTION
TEST 1

DIRECTIONS: Each question or incomplete statement is followed by several suggested answers or completions. Select the one that BEST answers the question or completes the statement. *PRINT THE LETTER OF THE CORRECT ANSWER IN THE SPACE AT THE RIGHT.*

1. A newly appointed maintainer, assigned to work with a more experienced maintainer, finds this experienced maintainer constantly violating the safety rules.
   The BEST thing for the new maintainer to do would be to

   A. say nothing to anyone since this maintainer is more experienced
   B. say nothing to this maintainer but report him to the foreman
   C. ask the foreman for another assignment before an accident occurs
   D. warn this maintainer that he is endangering his life and the lives of others

2. Unless specifically authorized by the superintendent, the minimum length of contact rail that may be installed is _____ feet.

   A. 55　　　　B. 39　　　　C. 26　　　　D. 10

3. Much power distribution work is done on live, rather than de-energized 600-volt equipment, PRIMARILY because

   A. the work can be done in less time
   B. 600 volts is not considered high voltage
   C. it is too difficult to de-energize the equipment
   D. it is desirable to keep traffic moving with minimum delay

4. When flagging on a curve, an intermediate flagman should give a proceed signal to the motorman with _____ flag(s).

   A. one white　　　　　　　B. two white
   C. one yellow　　　　　　 D. two yellow

5. The reason a bank of lights has five 120-volt lamps in series, rather than in parallel, is that

   A. a series circuit uses less wiring
   B. a series circuit is easier to maintain
   C. this allows the third rail to be used as a power source
   D. the same amount of power will be dissipated by the circuit and by the third rail

6. New maintenance instructions and procedures are periodically issued by the power distribution department for the purpose of

   A. evaluating employee performance
   B. guiding employees in their work
   C. reminding employees of their duties
   D. justifying penalties in case of errors in maintenance

7. After using a rubber mat, a RECOMMENDED practice that will extend its life is to

   A. wipe it clean
   B. spread it out to dry
   C. apply a light coat of oil to it
   D. fold it and place it in a tool box

8. Minor injuries sustained by an employee should be reported

   A. as soon as possible
   B. only if time is lost
   C. at the end of his work day
   D. at the end of his work week

9. With respect to flagging signals, the statement which is NOT true is that

   A. in an emergency, a red light may be used to give a proceed signal
   B. under normal flagging conditions, moving a white light up and down means proceed slowly
   C. in an emergency, any object waved violently by anyone on or near the track is a signal to the motorman to stop
   D. under normal flagging conditions, moving a red light across the track is the authorized stop signal

10. Where two rail bonds are used at each negative rail joint, and one bond breaks off at one terminal,

    A. all train service would be stopped in that area
    B. only half the regular train service could be maintained
    C. the remaining bond will fail at once due to overload
    D. normal train service could be maintained until repairs are made

11. Before installing a welded negative rail bond, the surface of the rail should be

    A. ground and scraped   B. tinned
    C. washed clean   D. grooved

12. If a contact rail does not rest properly on an insulator because the insulator is low, shims should be inserted BETWEEN the

    A. tie and insulator
    B. cap and contact rail
    C. insulator and cap
    D. centering cup and insulator

13. A slight coating of rust on small tools is BEST removed by

    A. rubbing the tool with a damp cloth
    B. scraping the tool with a sharp knife
    C. applying a heavy coat of vaseline to the tool
    D. rubbing the tool with kerosene and fine steel wool

14. The end of the protection board is required to overhang an end approach by _____ inches.

    A. 2   B. 3   C. 4   D. 6

15. The PRINCIPAL reason for NOT using your finger to align holes in two metal plates is that

    A. this is an unsafe practice
    B. this is not an accurate method
    C. your finger may be moist or greasy
    D. the holes are usually too small

16. All employees should have a copy of the rules and regulations.
    The MAIN reason for this is to

    A. give the answers to non-technical questions
    B. make employees responsible for their acts
    C. acquaint the employees with their duties and responsibilities
    D. relieve management of responsibility for certain actions that may occur

17. The third rail insulators are made of

    A. porcelain
    B. wood
    C. hard rubber
    D. asbestos block

18. A five-lamp series cluster which is connected to the third rail does not light after all five lamps have been replaced by new lamps.
    To make certain the trouble is localized in this particular cluster, a maintainer SHOULD

    A. test the circuit fuse at the lighting panel
    B. remove one lamp in the cluster and test to ground
    C. test each socket sheel to ground with a lamp bank
    D. observe whether other lamp clusters on the same rail are lighted

19. To prevent the drill from wandering when a hole is to be drilled in a steel rail, it is BEST to

    A. use a dull drill
    B. use a high speed drill
    C. exert heavy pressure when drilling
    D. center-punch the spot to be drilled

20. When connecting a portable tool to a live 600-volt D.C. circuit, the best procedure is to make the negative or ground connection first and then make the positive connection.
    The reason for this procedure is that

    A. there is less danger of accidental shock
    B. electricity flows from positive to negative
    C. the reverse procedure may blow the circuit breaker
    D. less arcing will occur when the connection is made

21. Heavy copper bonds between rail lengths indicate that this rail is carrying _____ current.

    A. stray
    B. signal
    C. positive feeder
    D. negative return

22. A blue light in the subway indicates the location of an emergency alarm box, a telephone and a(n)

   A. ladder
   B. first aid kit
   C. emergency exit
   D. fire extinguisher

23. In contact rail construction, brackets are used to support the

   A. protection board
   B. contact rail insulators
   C. centering cup
   D. contact rail ties

24. A maintainer opens the switch of a certain circuit on which he is going to work. The PROPER procedure to make sure that the circuit will not be made *alive* accidentally is to

   A. block the switch open and tag it
   B. ground both terminals of the switch
   C. inform his superior of the circumstances
   D. inform all maintainers who are working in the vicinity

25. When a tool is issued to a maintainer for use on the job, he is NOT held responsible for

   A. proper and correct use of the tool
   B. wear of the tool through normal use
   C. careful storage of the tool
   D. reasonable protection of the tool against loss

26. When drilling a rail for a compressed terminal bond, it should be drilled *dry* (without using oil).
   The BEST reason for this is that an undesirable film of oil

   A. might remain on the inside of the hole
   B. would cause the drill to become too hot
   C. would shorten the useful life of the rail
   D. might get on the top of the rail and cause wheels to slip

27. A circuit breaker is said to be *trip-free* if

   A. it will trip on overload
   B. it will trip on reverse current
   C. the tripping devices operate easily
   D. the closing and tripping operations are independent of each other

28. Before cable is pulled into a new underground duct, a mandrel should be passed through the duct.
   The purpose of this is to

   A. drain the duct of water
   B. measure the length of the duct
   C. clear the duct of obstructions
   D. draw the pulling rope through the duct

29. Good practice requires that cartridge fuses be removed from their clips with a fuse puller rather than with the bare hand in order to AVOID

    A. personal injury
    B. breakage of the fuse
    C. damage to the fuse clips
    D. the possibility of drawing an arc

30. With reference to contact rail jumpers and track rail bonds, it is CORRECT to say that

    A. both contact rail jumpers and track rail bonds are insulated
    B. neither contact rail jumpers nor track rail bonds are insulated
    C. contact rail jumpers are not insulated while track rail bonds are insulated
    D. contact rail jumpers are insulated while track rail bonds are not insulated

31. The type of knife switch normally installed in a tap from a contact rail is a _____ switch.

    A. TPST   B. DPDT   C. SPST   D. TPDT

32. When electric arc welding is done, the arc at the end of the welding rod is _____ voltage and _____ amperage.

    A. high; low
    B. low; high
    C. low; low
    D. high; high

33. When reporting a defective contact rail insulator in a subway section, the information that should be given so that it may be found readily is the track number and the

    A. stationing
    B. insulator number
    C. distance from the end of the section
    D. distance from the nearest passenger station

34. A *Cadweld* charge is ignited by a(n)

    A. long wooden matchstick
    B. oxyacetylene flame
    C. gas operated burner
    D. spark gun

35. The contact rail is prevented from moving lengthwise by

    A. anti-creepers
    B. anchors
    C. splice bars
    D. expansion joints

36. A large lag screw is MOST easily removed from a protection board with a _____ wrench.

    A. spanner   B. box   C. strap   D. stillson

37. Electric current is measured with a(n)

    A. ohmmeter
    B. voltmeter
    C. ammeter
    D. wattmeter

38. If a maintainer is assigned to walk alone while on an inspection trip along an underground right-of-way, it is MOST important for him to carry a

    A. whistle
    B. portable train stop
    C. lantern
    D. flag

39. A maintainer is entitled to a day off on his birthday. The PROPER procedure for him to follow would be to notify supervision _____ in advance.

    A. verbally at least one week
    B. verbally at least two days
    C. in writing at least one day
    D. in writing at least three days

40. When a maintainer presents a grievance to his immediate superior, it must be WITHIN _____ after the occurrence of the event complained of.

    A. 7 days   B. 5 days   C. 48 hours   D. 24 hours

KEY (CORRECT ANSWERS)

1. D	11. A	21. D	31. C
2. C	12. B	22. D	32. B
3. D	13. D	23. A	33. A
4. C	14. B	24. A	34. D
5. C	15. A	25. B	35. B
6. B	16. C	26. A	36. B
7. A	17. A	27. D	37. C
8. A	18. D	28. C	38. C
9. A	19. D	29. A	39. A
10. D	20. A	30. D	40. B

TEST 2

DIRECTIONS: Each question or incomplete statement is followed by several suggested answers or completions. Select the one that BEST answers the question or completes the statement. *PRINT THE LETTER OF THE CORRECT ANSWER IN THE SPACE AT THE RIGHT.*

Questions 1-4.

DIRECTIONS: Questions 1 through 4 are based on the rule preceding each question. Be sure to consider only the information given in the rule which IMMEDIATELY PRECEDES the question.

RULE: Transit employees who enter upon the subway tracks are not to wear loose fitting clothes.

1. The MOST important reason for this rule is that loose fitting clothing 1.____

    A. may catch on some projection of a passing train
    B. gives poor protection against electrical hazards
    C. does not keep dust and dirt from getting on the employees
    D. can interfere with the employee when he is moving equipment

RULE: In walking on the track, walk opposite the direction of traffic, if possible.

2. The LOGICAL reason for this rule is that the man on the track 2.____

    A. will be seen more readily by the motorman
    B. is better able to judge the speed of a train
    C. is more likely to see an approaching train
    D. will have more room to stand clear of a train

RULE: Employees are required to report defective equipment to their superiors, even when the maintenance of the particular equipment is handled by another department.

3. The PRIMARY purpose of this rule is to 3.____

    A. encourage alertness among employees
    B. reduce the possibility of an accident
    C. encourage all departments to work together
    D. place the responsibility within the proper department

RULE: Keys, metal key chains or metal clasps for key rings must not be worn on the outside of clothing.

4. The REASON for this rule is that 4.____

    A. employees may lose their keys
    B. these metal objects may get damaged and become unusable
    C. any light shining on these objects may be mistaken for a signal
    D. these metal objects may come in contact with live electrical equipment

5. Goggles are LEAST necessary when

   A. cutting angle iron with a torch
   B. grinding an end approach connection
   C. welding contact rail
   D. removing an insulator

6. The voltage level used to differentiate between low voltage and high voltage apparatus is _____ volts.

   A. 440   B. 600   C. 750   D. 1000

7. If a drawing for a contact rail installation is made to a scale of 1 1/2" to the foot, the drawing is said to be _____ size.

   A. one-sixteenth   B. one-eighth
   C. one-quarter   D. one-half

8. A *No Clearance* area along the subway's right-of-way is indicated by a sign that has diagonal stripes which are colored

   A. blue and white   B. blue and yellow
   C. red and white   D. red and blue

9. When working on live 600-volt equipment, a maintainer SHOULD

   A. carry a spare pair of rubber gloves
   B. wear rubber gloves over leather gloves
   C. wear leather gloves over rubber gloves
   D. reinforce the fingers or rubber gloves with rubber tape

10. Testing for a blown cartridge fuse by connecting a lamp across the suspected fuse will, IN ALL CASES, indicate a _____ fuse if the lamp _____.

    A. good; lights   B. blown; lights
    C. good; remains dark   D. blown; remains dark

11. The bridging of a fuse by a wire is PROHIBITED because the

    A. fuse will blow
    B. wire will overload the circuit
    C. person inserting the wire may receive a shock
    D. circuit will lose the protection afforded by the fuse

12. A contact rail insulator MUST be replaced if it is

    A. chipped   B. damp   C. dirty   D. old

13. On a section of four-track subway, pulling an emergency alarm box will USUALLY kill the contact rail on

    A. all four tracks   B. the nearest track only
    C. the local tracks only   D. the express tracks only

14. In contact rail insulator installations, the PURPOSE of the centering cup is to

    A. hold the insulator in place
    B. drain moisture from the insulator

C. reduce vibrations in the contact rail
D. prevent the lag screw from cutting into the tie

15. A portable train stop should be used in connection with flagging operations ONLY

    A. at crossovers
    B. when proper signal lanterns are not available
    C. if the flagman believes the motorman will not stop
    D. after caution lights or flags have been properly displayed

16. Jumper cable connections to the contact rail SHOULD be installed

    A. *without* slack, to save material
    B. *without* slack, to avoid a tripping hazard
    C. *with* slack, to avoid strain due to rail movement
    D. *with* slack, to allow for cable contraction in cold weather

17. Before using a portable electric grinder in the field, the POSITIVE connection to the contact rail should be made _____ the negative connection and removed _____ the negative connection is removed.

    A. after; after
    B. after; before
    C. before; after
    D. before; before

18. Power supply connections to the contact rail are made through switches, fuses, or circuit breakers. Circuit breakers should ALWAYS be used when

    A. the circuit is not de-energized often
    B. there is a circuit breaker house in the vicinity
    C. protection against instantaneous overloads is essential
    D. the switching device must be operated from a distant point

19. General safety instructions state that an employee walking on the tracks in the subway should ALWAYS

    A. stay away from *No Clearance* areas
    B. take the shortest route between two points
    C. walk as close to the protection board as possible
    D. expect trains to run at any time, on any track, and in any direction

20. End approaches are used to

    A. disconnect car shoes from the contact rail
    B. lift car shoes onto a section of the contact rail
    C. ease car shoes over cable connections to the contact rail
    D. reduce pressure of the car shoes on the contact rail at crossings

21. It would be MOST important for a maintainer to take immediate action if he found a

    A. cracked running rail
    B. burned out tunnel light
    C. broken running rail bond
    D. leak in a signal air line

22. If it is necessary for you to do some work with your hands under a piece of heavy equipment while a fellow worker lifts up and holds one end of it by means of a pinch bar, the MOST important safety precaution that should be taken is to

    A. wear work gloves
    B. work as fast as possible
    C. insert a temporary block to support the equipment
    D. watch the bar and be ready to get clear if it slips

23. Friction tape should be applied to a cable splice with

    A. a one-quarter lap
    B. a one-half lap
    C. a three-quarter lap
    D. adjacent edges butting

24. The FUNCTION of the gap or series breaker in a contact rail section is to

    A. sectionalize the line
    B. insure continuous current to the rail section
    C. protect against overloading an adjacent section
    D. equalize the load on the various rails in the section

25. The minimum number of lanterns required to properly protect a crew of power distribution employees working in the subway is five.
    The colors of these lanterns should be _____ green, _____ yellow, _____ red, and _____ white.

    A. two; one; one; one
    B. one; two; one; one
    C. one; one; two; one
    D. one; one; one; two

26. Rubber mats must be used when working on contact rail installation because the ground may be

    A. rough   B. damp   C. sloped   D. dirty

27. A COMMON defect in cold chisels which makes them unsafe for use is a

    A. shortened shank
    B. dull cutting edge
    C. mushroomed head
    D. sharp cutting edge

28. Cleats are used in connection with D.C. cable supports to

    A. reduce vibration
    B. make installation easier
    C. distribute the load more evenly
    D. prevent damage to the cable covering

29. Contact rails are sectionalized.
    The PURPOSE of this is to

    A. reduce power consumption
    B. limit the effect of a fault
    C. permit the use of lighter rails
    D. make it safer for maintenance gangs to repair rails

30. Employees are cautioned not to use water to extinguish fires involving live electrical equipment.
    The MAIN reason for this is that water

    A. may damage wire insulation
    B. may transmit a shock to the user
    C. will not extinguish an electrical fire
    D. will turn to steam and make it difficult to fight the fire

31. A flagman hears a motorman sound two long blasts on his horn.
    This means the motorman is

    A. passing caution lights
    B. going to apply his brakes
    C. requesting assistance
    D. answering a flagman's signal

32. The pry bar GENERALLY used to lift the contact rail when replacing an insulator is made of wood because wood is

    A. a non-conductor
    B. less expensive than metal
    C. not hard enough to damage the rail
    D. less likely to bend under pressure

33. When a maintainer telephones to give advance notice of his intention to be absent, the LEAST important information he could give is

    A. his home address
    B. his name and pass number
    C. the reason for his absence
    D. when he expects to return to work

34. When installing switches for connections to the contact rail, it is LEAST important that the switch box be so located that it will

    A. be readily accessible
    B. require a minimum of cable
    C. be close to the contact rail
    D. not interfere with train clearance requirements

35. An electric hand tool should not be lifted or carried by its service cord PRIMARILY because

    A. the cord might pull off its terminals
    B. a secure grip cannot be obtained on the cord
    C. the rubber covering on the cord might be overstretched
    D. the tool would swing and be damaged by striking some hard object

36. The PROPER procedure to use in order to make sure that a 600-volt circuit is dead is to

    A. ground the circuit
    B. check if the fuses are warm
    C. test it with a bank of lights
    D. touch it quickly with your finger

37. In an accident report, the information which is MOST useful in decreasing the recurrence of similar type accidents is the

    A. cause of the accident
    B. number of people involved
    C. time the accident happened
    D. extent of injuries sustained

38. While acting as a flagman protecting a gang working on the track, a maintainer should give the *proceed* signal to the motorman

    A. immediately after the maintainer blows his whistle
    B. only after the motorman brings the train to a complete stop
    C. as soon as the motorman gives the maintainer the proper signal
    D. when the employee in charge indicates that the men and the track are clear

39. When orally reporting minor trouble to your foreman, the MOST important information the foreman would require from you would be

    A. how the trouble started
    B. how the trouble can be resolved
    C. the exact time you discovered the trouble
    D. the type of trouble and its exact location

40. When a job on the track is finished and the flagging protection is to be removed, the LAST item removed should be the

    A. white flag or light
    B. green flag or light
    C. portable train stop
    D. red flag or light

KEY (CORRECT ANSWERS)

1. A	11. D	21. A	31. A
2. C	12. A	22. C	32. A
3. B	13. A	23. B	33. A
4. D	14. A	24. A	34. C
5. D	15. D	25. B	35. A
6. C	16. C	26. B	36. C
7. B	17. B	27. C	37. A
8. C	18. D	28. D	38. D
9. C	19. D	29. B	39. D
10. B	20. B	30. B	40. B

EXAMINATION SECTION
TEST 1

DIRECTIONS: Each question or incomplete statement is followed by several suggested answers or completions. Select the one that BEST answers the question or completes the statement. *PRINT THE LETTER OF THE CORRECT ANSWER IN THE SPACE AT THE RIGHT.*

1. In power distribution maintenance, much of the work is done on live 600 volt equipment PRIMARILY because   1.____

    A. 600 volts will not cause a serious electric shock
    B. power distribution employees are safety conscious
    C. it is very difficult to de-energize the equipment
    D. it is desirable to keep traffic moving with minimum delay

2. The location of an emergency alarm box in the subway is indicated by a _____ light.   2.____

    A. red   B. green   C. blue   D. amber

3. Electric arc welding is COMMONLY done with _____ voltage and _____ amperage.   3.____

    A. low; high
    C. high; low
    B. low; low
    D. high; high

4. When leather gloves are worn over rubber gloves, the MAIN purpose of the leather gloves is to   4.____

    A. provide additional insulation
    B. protect the rubber gloves from mechanical injury
    C. provide a more secure grip on tools
    D. keep the rubber gloves clean

5. Side approaches are USUALLY installed on the contact rail at   5.____

    A. turnouts
    B. each end of all station platforms
    C. the ends of all rail sections
    D. feed points

6. In general, bonds are NOT connected to rails by means of _____ terminals.   6.____

    A. welded   B. expanded   C. bolted   D. compressed

7. A knife switch installed in a tap from a contact rail would NORMALLY be a _____ switch.   7.____

    A. TPST   B. DPDT   C. TPDT   D. SPST

8. In most sections of the subway, one track rail carries the negative return current and the other rail is used for signal circuits.
The QUICKEST way of identifying the rail carrying the negative return current is to look for   8.____

    A. signs of arcing on the top surface of the rail
    B. heavy copper bonds between rail lengths

25

C. insulating segments between rail sections
D. expansion gaps between rail lengths

9. When using a portable electric tool, it is good practice to have the tool frame grounded to   9.____

   A. reduce current leakage from the armature
   B. prevent short circuits
   C. reduce the danger of overheating
   D. prevent the frame from becoming live to ground

10. When a job on the track is finished and the flagging protection is to be removed, the   10.____
    FIRST item removed should be the

    A. white flag or light   B. portable train stop
    C. red flag or light   D. green flag or light

11. If your foreman gave you a job to be done in a certain way and after starting the job you   11.____
    think of another method that you are convinced is better, you should

    A. follow the method given by the foreman since he would probably reject your idea
    B. try your own method since the foreman probably would not know the difference
    C. request the foreman's opinion of your method before proceeding further
    D. obtain the opinion of another maintainer and act accordingly

12. According to the Book of Rules, employees, while on system property, may indulge in   12.____
    card playing

    A. at no time
    B. only during the lunch period
    C. when not actively performing their duties
    D. just before or after working hours

13. When contact rail lengths are bonded rigidly with welded copper bonds, it is always necessary to provide   13.____

    A. special insulated supports at each joint
    B. expansion joints at certain intervals
    C. a rigid connection between rail and each insulator
    D. auxiliary protective sleeves on the bonds

14. Before installing a third rail clamp connecting a cable to the third rail, the rail surface   14.____
    should be

    A. tinned with solder
    B. washed with a weak acid solution
    C. bevelled with a rough file
    D. cleaned by scraping or grinding

15. When the track has cleared at a work location, a flagman should signal the motorman to   15.____
    proceed.
    This proceed signal must NEVER be given with

    A. the hand   B. a white lamp
    C. a yellow lamp   D. a red lamp

16. The function of a gap or series breaker in a contact rail section is to   16.____

   A. protect against overloading an adjacent section
   B. equalize the load on the various rails
   C. sectionalize the line
   D. connect the substation to the rail

17. Usually a porcelain rather than a wood cable cleat is used   17.____

   A. at a wet location
   B. where there is much vibration
   C. on elevated structures
   D. where extra strength is required

18. The tip of a soldering iron is made of copper because   18.____

   A. solder will not stick to other metals
   B. copper is a very good conductor of heat
   C. it is easily cleaned
   D. the melting point of copper is very high

19. Blowout coils on heavy duty contactors are used to   19.____

   A. prevent fuse failure
   B. help extinguish the arc when the circuit is opened
   C. sound an alarm when circuit is shorted
   D. extinguish the arc when the circuit is closed

20. The information needed when ordering incandescent lamps is the   20.____

   A. amperage and whether A.C. or D.C.
   B. amperage and wattage
   C. voltage and whether A.C. or D.C.
   D. voltage and wattage

21. Ferrule-contact type cartridge fuses are for currents NOT exceeding _____ amperes.   21.____

   A. 30   B. 60   C. 100   D. 600

22. When the term No. 3 is used in connection with sandpaper, it refers to the   22.____

   A. size of the sheet
   B. thickness of the paper
   C. fineness of the abrasive
   D. weight of the paper

23. If two contactors are so connected that serious trouble would result if they were both closed at the same time, they are USUALLY provided with   23.____

   A. a quick break feature   B. interlocks
   C. protective resistors   D. time delay elements

24. With respect to the safety value of insulation on tools, it can be properly said that the insulation

   A. should not be used as the only protective measure
   B. provides very little real protection
   C. is of value mainly to the new helper
   D. insures the safety of the user

25. The abbreviation R.I.W.P. is used to describe a type of

   A. contact rail   B. breaker
   C. conduit   D. cable

26. Heavy duty resistor grids are COMMONLY made of

   A. aluminum   B. brass   C. copper   D. iron

27. Comparing No. 18 gage and No. 12 gage bare copper wire of equal lengths, the No. 18 gage will have GREATER

   A. conductivity   B. resistance
   C. strength   D. weight

28. The voltage across a burned out lamp in a series cluster of five lamps when connected across 600 volts D.C. is

   A. 600   B. 480   C. 120   D. 0

29. To connect a 2,000,000 c.m. feeder cable to four 500,000 c.m. cables, the usual method is to

   A. make a special sweated splice
   B. bolt all cables to a flat copper plate
   C. use a mechanical connector
   D. pair the smaller cables and make two splices

30. Before cable is pulled into a new underground duct, a wooden mandrel should be passed through the duct. The purpose of this is to

   A. drain the duct of water
   B. measure the length of the duct
   C. clear the duct of obstructions
   D. draw the pulling rope through the duct

31. The vertical distance between the contact surface of the contact rail and the top of the running rail is the

   A. elevation   B. horizontal gage
   C. clearance   D. easement

32. It is important to make certain that a ladle is free of water before using it to scoop up molten solder since water may

   A. cool the solder
   B. dilute the solder
   C. prevent the solder from sticking
   D. cause the solder to splatter

33. TA specifications require that metal conduits be galvanized. The reason for this is that galvanizing will

    A. reduce sweating
    B. reduce heating
    C. add mechanical strength
    D. retard corrosion

34. If the allowable current density for copper bus bar is 900 amperes per square inch, the current carrying capacity, in amperes, of a bar 1/4" x 3" and 12 feet long is

    A. 675   B. 900   C. 1200   D. 8100

35. Testing for a blown cartridge fuse by connecting a lamp across the suspected fuse will in all cases indicate a _____ fuse if the lamp _____.

    A. blown; lights
    B. good; remains dark
    C. blown; remains dark
    D. good; lights

36. Twenty boxes full of bolts weigh 500 pounds, and each box when empty weighs 2 pounds.
The total weight of the bolts is _____ pounds.

    A. 450   B. 460   C. 506   D. 540

37. A breaker is said to be trip free if

    A. the tripping devices operate easily
    B. it will trip on reverse current
    C. the closing and tripping operations are independent
    D. it will trip on overload

38. In melting solder, the formation of excessive dross is an indication that

    A. the solder temperature is too low
    B. the tin content of the solder is too high
    C. too much heat is being applied
    D. the tin content of the solder is too low

39. As a rule, the subway fans are in use ONLY

    A. when the contact rail has been de-energized due to trouble
    B. on very warm days
    C. on very cold days
    D. during the rush hour

40. A typical equalizer breaker between two sections of contact rail has _____ trip(s).

    A. an overload
    B. a reverse current
    C. both overload and reverse current
    D. neither overload nor reverse current

KEY (CORRECT ANSWERS)

1. D	11. C	21. B	31. A
2. C	12. A	22. C	32. D
3. A	13. B	23. B	33. D
4. B	14. D	24. A	34. A
5. A	15. D	25. D	35. A
6. C	16. C	26. D	36. B
7. D	17. A	27. B	37. C
8. B	18. B	28. A	38. C
9. D	19. B	29. C	39. A
10. B	20. D	30. C	40. A

TEST 2

DIRECTIONS: Each question or incomplete statement is followed by several suggested answers or completions. Select the one that BEST answers the question or completes the statement. *PRINT THE LETTER OF THE CORRECT ANSWER IN THE SPACE AT THE RIGHT.*

1. Contact rail weights are USUALLY given in pounds per   1.____

   A. 33 foot lengths B. inch
   C. foot D. yard

2. The MAIN purpose of the carbons in an air circuit breaker is to   2.____

   A. increase the capacity of the breaker
   B. prevent burning of the main contacts
   C. prevent flashover
   D. prevent violent opening

3. Protection boards in the subway are fastened to their brackets by means of   3.____

   A. lag screws B. clamps
   C. nuts and bolts D. rivets

4. The MAIN difference between a quick-break knife switch and a standard knife switch is that a quick-break switch   4.____

   A. has a spring-operated auxiliary blade attached to the main blade
   B. has a coil spring at the hinge to assist in quick opening
   C. requires less tension at the clips
   D. can be more easily adapted for operation by remote control

5. On a section of a four-track subway, pulling an emergency alarm box will usually de-energize the contact rail on   5.____

   A. the nearest track only B. all four tracks
   C. the express tracks only D. the local tracks only

6. Good practice requires that cartridge fuses be removed from their clips with a fuse puller rather than with the bare hand to avoid   6.____

   A. breakage of the fuse
   B. personal injury
   C. damage to the fuse clips
   D. the possibility of drawing an arc

7. Suppose that a fellow employee has lost his pass and asks you to lend him your pass to be used to perform an errand for the foreman.   7.____
   You should

   A. refuse because you might need the pass yourself
   B. lend the pass if the foreman approves
   C. refuse because the pass is issued for your own use only
   D. lend the pass because it is going to be used on a legitimate errand

8. Periodic cleaning inspection and testing of power distribution equipment is done MAINLY to

   A. check to see if the equipment was properly installed
   B. familiarize employees with the type of equipment in service
   C. diminish the chances of equipment failing when in service
   D. determine if the equipment should be replaced by more efficient equipment

9. The bridging of a fuse by a wire is prohibited because the

   A. fuse will blow
   B. wire will overload the circuit
   C. circuit will lose the protection afforded by the fuse
   D. person inserting the wire may receive a shock

10. When a 1:2:4 mix of concrete is specified, the 2 indicates the proportion of

    A. water   B. sand   C. stone   D. cement

11. A power distribution maintainer's work is USUALLY done close to 600 volt equipment. A good general safety course for him to follow is to

    A. wear rubber gloves at all times
    B. test all equipment in the vicinity before starting any work
    C. never work on any electrical equipment unless it is grounded
    D. consider all electrical equipment energized unless he definitely knows otherwise

12. The sum of the following dimensions: 3' 2 1/4", 8 7/8", 2' 6 3/8", 2' 9 3/4", and 1' 0" is

    A. 9' 3 1/4"   B. 10' 3 1/4"   C. 10' 7 1/4"   D. 16' 7 1/4"

13. If a drawing for a contact rail installation is made to a scale of 1 1/2" to the foot, the drawing is said to be one _____ size.

    A. sixteenth   B. eighth   C. quarter   D. half

14. Jumper cable connections to the contact rail should be installed

    A. with slack, to avoid strain due to rail movement
    B. without slack, to avoid a tripping hazard
    C. without slack, to save material
    D. with slack, to allow for cable contraction in cold weather

15. A D.C. air circuit breaker is adjusted so that the

    A. main and arcing contacts open simultaneously
    B. arcing contacts open before the main contacts
    C. main contacts close before the arcing contacts
    D. main contacts open before the arcing contacts

16. In case of a violent short circuit between the third rail and the negative rail, the circuit breakers that would normally open would be the _____ feeder breakers and _____ breakers.

    A. substation; track feeder
    B. track; equalizer

C. substation; equalizer
D. track feeder breaker, substation; equalizer

17. A contact rail insulator should NOT be installed on the tie supporting a running rail joint because the

   A. insulator would interfere with the installation of negative bonds
   B. joint would make replacement of the insulator difficult
   C. insulator bolt hole would weaken the tie
   D. insulator might be damaged by vibration

18. If a negative rail bond should become grounded,

   A. there would be no immediate noticeable effect
   B. the bond would immediately burn off the rail
   C. trains would come to a stop in the section
   D. the feeder and equalizer breakers on the section would trip

19. Immediate action would be required on the part of a TA employee if he found

   A. a burnt out tunnel light
   B. a cracked running rail
   C. a broken running rail bond
   D. any leak on a signal air line

20. General safety instructions state that an employee in the subway should always

   A. carry a first aid kit
   B. be accompanied by a foreman
   C. carry a complete set of lamps
   D. expect trains to run at any time on any track and in any direction

21. Welded negative rail bonds are USUALLY attached to the _____ side of the rail _____.

   A. outer; head   B. inner; head
   C. outer; web   D. inner; web

22. Some power supply connections to the contact rail are made through knife switches and fuses, others through circuit breakers.
   Circuit breakers would always be used when

   A. the switching device must be operated from a distant point
   B. there is a circuit breaker house in the vicinity
   C. the circuit is seldom de-energized
   D. the circuit must be protected against overloads

23. The centering cup used to hold the contact rail insulator in place is fastened to its supporting tie by means of a

   A. hook bolt   B. machine screw
   C. lag screw   D. spike

24. Track equalizer breakers, feeder breakers, and gap breakers are normally operated by remote control by the

    A. power department
    B. power distribution department
    C. track department
    D. trainmaster

25. When installing lag screws,

    A. the screws should be given an extra turn after the heads are properly seated
    B. holes slightly smaller than the screws should first be drilled into the wood
    C. the screws should be driven by striking with a hammer
    D. the screws should first be dipped in light oil

26. When using a portable electric grinder in the field, you should make the positive connection to the contact rail _____ the negative and remove it _____ the negative.

    A. after; after
    B. before; after
    C. after; before
    D. before; before

27. A corroded or poor electrical connection in a circuit generally has a tendency to develop a high spot temperature.
    This is because the bad connection

    A. increases the flow of current through the connection
    B. decreases the effective resistance of the connection
    C. increases the voltage drop across the connection
    D. decreases the voltage drop across the connections

28. At a standard double crossover in the subway, the required number of side approaches is

    A. 2   B. 4   C. 6   D. 8

29. A good precaution that will extend the life of rubber mats is to

    A. periodically apply a light coat of oil
    B. fold them carefully and place them at the bottom of the tool box
    C. spread them out to dry in the sun when they are wet
    D. wipe them clean after using

30. When a new end approach is fitted to a worn contact rail, to make the two surfaces flush and smooth at the joint, the usual practice is to

    A. grind the top surface of the approach to fit
    B. use a special low insulator for the approach
    C. use a special high insulator for the rail
    D. raise the worn rail with shims

31. The wood used for protection board is MAINLY

    A. pine   B. oak   C. maple   D. walnut

32. Concealed or inside negative bonds are

    A. connected under the base of the rail
    B. made of insulated cable
    C. always connected on the inside of the rail
    D. installed between the joint bars and the rail

33. When installing contact rail and protection board on curves,

    A. both the rail and board are curved
    B. short lengths of both rail and board are used
    C. only the rail is curved
    D. regular lengths of board and short lengths of rail are used

34. Contact rail jumper cables are USUALLY installed at

    A. all rail joints
    B. points where the contact rail is transposed
    C. section breaks or gaps
    D. feeder connections

35. When a compressed terminal bond is being installed, it is MOST important that the holes drilled in the rail be

    A. free of grease or moisture
    B. tapered
    C. under size
    D. oiled lightly

36. When reporting a defective contact rail insulator in a subway section, the information that should be given so that it may be found readily is the track number and the

    A. stationing
    B. distance from the nearest passenger station
    C. distance from the end of the section
    D. insulator number

37. One good reason for using lead in solder is because lead has

    A. high density   B. flexibility
    C. a low melting point   D. low resistance

38. In track rail bonding, clamp bonds would be used

    A. between ends of guard rails
    B. from guard rail to main rail
    C. between ends of negative rails
    D. where no guard rail is installed

39. When applying friction tape to a cable splice, it should be applied with

    A. adjacent edges butting   B. one-quarter lap
    C. one-half lap   D. three-quarter lap

40. The purpose of an end approach is to
   A. operate annunciators when approaching a passenger station
   B. reduce the pressure of the car shoes on the contact rail at crossings
   C. ease the car shoes over cable connections to the contact rail
   D. lift the car shoes on to a section of the contact rail

KEY (CORRECT ANSWERS)

1. D	11. D	21. A	31. A
2. B	12. B	22. A	32. D
3. C	13. B	23. C	33. C
4. A	14. A	24. A	34. B
5. B	15. D	25. B	35. A
6. B	16. C	26. C	36. A
7. C	17. D	27. C	37. C
8. C	18. A	28. B	38. B
9. C	19. B	29. D	39. C
10. B	20. D	30. A	40. D

EXAMINATION SECTION
TEST 1

DIRECTIONS: Each question or incomplete statement is followed by several suggested answers or completions. Select the one that BEST answers the question or completes the statement. *PRINT THE LETTER OF THE CORRECT ANSWER IN THE SPACE AT THE RIGHT.*

1. Excessive humming of a magnetic contactor is MOST likely due to

    A. imperfect sealing of the magnet
    B. corroded current carrying contacts
    C. insufficient operating voltage
    D. an opening in the holding coil circuit

    1.____

2. A certain circuit requires a maximum of 10 amperes to operate properly.
   If a calibrated ammeter in the circuit reads 12 amperes, it is MOST probable that

    A. the ground connection is open
    B. one of the branch circuits is open
    C. a partial short exists somewhere in the circuit
    D. a high resistance connection exists somewhere in the circuit

    2.____

3. When a fire in a substation cannot be put out with the fire extinguishing equipment on hand, the safety rules require you to

    A. call the fire department
    B. shut down the substation immediately
    C. notify system operation at once
    D. ask the nearest substation for assistance

    3.____

4. The sensitivity of a D.C. voltmeter is expressed by the

    A. size of the voltmeter
    B. number of ohms per volt
    C. type of binding posts
    D. number and type of scale divisions

    4.____

5. The word *plan,* when used on a blueprint, indicates a

    A. front elevation view
    B. side elevation view
    C. top view
    D. systematic order of assembly

    5.____

6. If the input to a 2:1 step-down transformer is 10 amperes at 440 volts, the output will be MOST NEARLY _____ amperes at _____ volts.

    A. 5; 220   B. 5; 380   C. 20; 220   D. 20; 880

    6.____

7. Alternating current equipment is usually rated in kva while direct current equipment is rated in kw.
   The reason for this is that

    7.____

A. D.C. equipment is less accurate than A.C. equipment
B. A.C. has a reactive current which also causes heating
C. A.C. equipment uses higher voltages than D.C. equipment
D. in a three-phase A.C. circuit, it is difficult to measure kw

8. A single-phase motor operating at 90% efficiency at full load is connected to a 220-volt source, and takes 10 amperes at 80% power factor.
The power delivered by the motor is APPROXIMATELY _____ watts.

   A. 1,585   B. 1,760   C. 1,955   D. 1,980

9. Five resistors, each having a different current rating, are connected in series. If the resistors are not to be overloaded, the MAXIMUM current permissible in the circuit is determined by the

A. resistor with the lowest current rating
B. resistor with the highest current rating
C. average current rating of the five resistors
D. sum of the current ratings of the five resistors

10. The device that creates the optical illusion of stopping the motion of a moving object by illuminating it with flashes of light at regular intervals is called a(n)

A. stroboscope   B. synchroscope
C. spectroscope   D. oscilloscope

11. Employees are not to walk, stand, or sit in the track area EXCEPT when

A. very tired
B. on a work break
C. waiting for materials to be delivered
D. necessary for the performance of their duties

12. When necessary to work on energized circuits, all *improperly* insulated tools

A. should only be used with rubber gloves
B. should not be used under any circumstances
C. should not be used except in emergency situations
D. can be used but should be replaced as soon as possible

13. A megger is an instrument that is used to measure

A. ampere-hours   B. insulation resistance
C. frequency   D. illumination

14. When working on the tracks, a bank of lights should be grounded to the

A. signal rail   B. nearest column
C. negative return rail   D. nearest lighting pipe

15. With respect to ladders, there is nothing wrong with the practice of

A. placing a ladder in front of an unlocked door
B. facing a ladder while climbing either up or down
C. reaching out from a ladder more than an arm's length
D. skipping over a broken rung when climbing up a ladder

16. The fuse in a certain circuit has blown and is replaced with a fuse of the same rating which also blows when the switch is closed.
   In this case,

   A. the circuit should be checked
   B. a fuse of higher current rating should be used
   C. a fuse of higher voltage rating should be used
   D. the fuse should be temporarily replaced by a heavy piece of wire

17. A standard knife switch carrying a D.C. load should be opened

   A. *rapidly,* to avoid blowing the fuse
   B. *rapidly,* to extinguish the arc quickly
   C. *slowly,* to permit the current to *die* slowly
   D. *slowly,* to avoid possible mechanical damage to the switch

Questions 18-25.

DIRECTIONS: Questions 18 through 25, inclusive, refer to Column I and Column II below. For each abbreviation, word, or phrase listed in Column I, select the item listed in Column II to which it BEST applies. In your answer space, next to the corresponding numbered question space, fill in your selected answer.

COLUMN I	COLUMN II
18. PILC	A. Wire or cable
19. Cartridge	B. Switch
20. DPDT	C. Battery
21. Hydrometer	D. Fuse or circuit breaker
22. Trip-free	
23. Ampere-hour	
24. Wheatstone Bridge	
25. Circular mil	

26. The reason for connecting the negative or ground wire before the positive wire when connecting a portable tool to a live 600-volt D.C. circuit is that

   A. the reverse procedure may blow the fuse
   B. there is less danger of accidental shock
   C. electricity flows from positive to negative
   D. less arcing will occur when the connection is made

27. A new maintainer has been assigned to a certain job and told that it must be finished by a certain time.
   If, after working for some time, he realizes that he cannot finish the job in time, he should

A. notify his foreman immediately
B. skip what he considers minor parts of the job
C. continue working and get as much done as possible
D. take it easy since the job cannot be done in time

28. To prevent a circuit from becoming energized accidentally after opening a switch, a maintainer should

   A. block the switch open and tag it
   B. ground both terminals of the switch
   C. notify his foreman that the switch is open
   D. tell all maintainers in the vicinity not to touch the switch

29. When a tool is issued to a maintainer for use on the job, he is NOT held responsible for

   A. careful storage of the tool
   B. proper and correct use of the tool
   C. wear of the tool through normal use
   D. reasonable protection of the tool against loss

30. The device often connected across relay contacts to minimize arcing when the contacts open is a

   A. spring   B. resistor
   C. capacitor   D. transistor

31. If the input to a motor-generator set is 1500 watts and the motor and generator losses total 250 watts, the efficiency of the set is MOST NEARLY

   A. 90%   B. 86%   C. 83%   D. 80%

Questions 32-38.

DIRECTIONS: Questions 32 through 38, inclusive, refer to the following circuit. Unless otherwise stated, ALL SWITCHES ARE CLOSED. Neglect the effects of the various meters on the circuit.

NOTE: $R_1 = R_3 = R_4 = 5$ ohms. $R_2 = R_5 = 10$ ohms

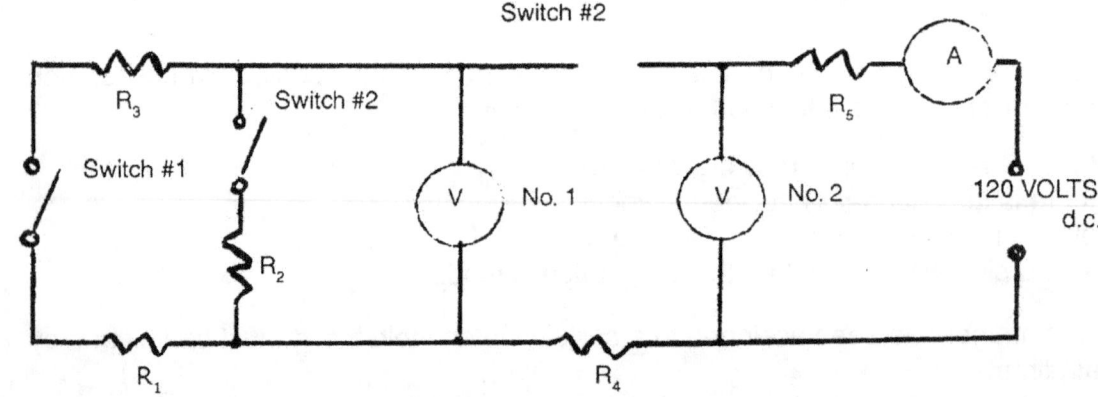

32. The equivalent resistance of the circuit is _____ ohms.

   A. 15   B. 20   C. 25   D. 35

33. The current through the ammeter is _____ amperes. 33.____
    A. 6   B. 12   C. 24   D. 30

34. Voltmeter No. 1 indicates _____ volts. 34.____
    A. 120   B. 90   C. 60   D. 30

35. The resistor that dissipates the same amount of power as R_1 is 35.____
    A. R_5 B. R_4 C. R_3 D. R_2

36. The voltage drop across R_1 is _____ volts. 36.____
    A. 75   B. 60   C. 30   D. 15

37. If the two lead wires to the ammeter are reversed, the 37.____
    A. ammeter will indicate zero current
    B. ammeter needle will move backwards
    C. current in the circuit will be reversed
    D. ammeter will continue to indicate properly

38. If Switches No. 1 and 2 are opened, voltmeter No. _____ will indicate _____ volts. 38.____
    A. 2; 0   B. 1; 0   C. 1; 120   D. 2; 60

39. The proper arrangement of the following wire sizes, in order of DECREASING resistance, is 39.____
    A. 1/0; 4/0; 2   B. 4/0; 1/0; 2
    C. 2; 4/0; 1/0   D. 2; 1/0; 4/0

40. Before disconnecting an ammeter from an energized current transformer circuit, the current transformer _____ should be _____. 40.____
    A. primary; shorted   B. secondary; shorted
    C. primary; opened   D. secondary; opened

KEY (CORRECT ANSWERS)

1. A	11. D	21. C	31. C
2. C	12. B	22. D	32. B
3. C	13. B	23. C	33. A
4. B	14. C	24. A	34. D
5. C	15. B	25. A	35. C
6. C	16. A	26. B	36. D
7. B	17. B	27. A	37. B
8. A	18. A	28. A	38. C
9. A	19. D	29. C	39. D
10. A	20. B	30. C	40. B

TEST 2

DIRECTIONS: Each question or incomplete statement is followed by several suggested answers or completions. Select the one that BEST answers the question or completes the statement. *PRINT THE LETTER OF THE CORRECT ANSWER IN THE SPACE AT THE RIGHT.*

1. If a self-excited motor-generator comes up to the rated speed but fails to build up generator voltage on the initial start, the FIRST thing to do is to   1._____

   A. increase the field resistance
   B. increase the speed of the motor
   C. check the armature insulation resistance
   D. reverse the connections to the shunt field

2. On a certain voltmeter, the same scale is used for three ranges; these are 0-750, 0-300, and 0-15 volts.   2._____
   If the scale is marked only for the 0-750 volt range, a scale reading of 300 when the 0-300 volt range is being used corresponds to an ACTUAL voltage of _____ volts.

   A. 15   B. 120   C. 225   D. 300

3. The flow of sufficient current to give positive action to protective lead sheath relays is insured by   3._____

   A. proper loading of the feeders
   B. the bonding together of cable lead sheaths
   C. providing more feeders than are required to carry the load
   D. connecting the metering equipment and the protective relays in series

4. A single-phase potential of 240 volts is required for test purposes. A 600-volt source and two identical transformers with 600-volt primary windings and 120-volt secondary windings are available.   4._____
   To get the required 240 volts, the transformers should be connected with the primaries in _____, secondaries in _____

   A. parallel; parallel   B. series; series
   C. series; parallel   D. parallel; series

5. The SMALLEST number of single-phase A.C. wattmeters required to measure the total power in a three-phase, 4-wire, unbalanced A.C. circuit is   5._____

   A. 1   B. 2   C. 3   D. 4

6. When both fuses and thermal cut-outs are used in a motor circuit, the   6._____

   A. fuses should be rated lower than the thermal cut-outs
   B. fuses are used to protect against continuous but not large overloads
   C. thermal cut-outs are used to protect against continuous overloads
   D. thermal cut-outs are used to protect against short circuits in the motor and branch circuits

7. A purpose of the green and red indicating lamps on a high tension feeder control panel is to indicate whether the   7._____

A. circuit breaker is opened or closed
B. control circuit is opened or closed
C. trip coil is energized or de-energized
D. closing coil is energized or de-energized

8. A D.C. relay that has its armature magnetically coupled with a permanent magnet is called a _____ relay.

    A. slow acting
    B. quick acting
    C. polarized
    D. rotating disc

9. Of the following devices, the one NOT used to change A.C. to D.C. is a(n)

    A. silicon rectifier
    B. ignitron
    C. motor-generator set
    D. battery

10. A transformer having only one winding is called a(n) _____ transformer.

    A. auto-
    B. potential
    C. constant-current
    D. split-phase

11. In electrical work, the symbol Hz stands for

    A. cycles per second
    B. watts per hour
    C. horsepower
    D. high voltage

12. The 110-volt bus supplying the control power in a substation is often D.C. from storage batteries charged automatically rather than A.C. from a transformer using the A.C. main supply.
One reason is that the D.C. system

    A. requires less maintenance
    B. is more reliable
    C. requires less power
    D. permits smaller control wires

13. Transistors have replaced vacuum tubes in many electronic applications.
One reason for this is that transistors

    A. can be used for higher voltages
    B. are larger
    C. cannot become defective
    D. require less power

14. The sum of the following dimensions: 12'11 3/16", 9'8 5/8", 7'3 3/4", 5'2 1/2", and 3'1 1/4" is

    A. 39'5 9/16"   B. 38'3 5/16"   C. 36'2 3/8"   D. 35'1 7/8"

15. Two common transformer voltage ratios used are

    A. 11,000/600 and 208/600
    B. 550/120 and 440/220
    C. 440/600 and 110/440
    D. 120/11,000 and 208/550

16. The MAIN purpose of the carbons in an air circuit breaker is to

    A. prevent flashover
    B. increase breaker capacity
    C. prevent a violent breaker opening
    D. prevent burning of the main contacts

17. If the scale on a drawing is 1/4" to the foot, then a 5/8" measurement would represent an ACTUAL length of

   A. 5'4"   B. 4'8"   C. 2'6"   D. 1'3"

Questions 18-22.

DIRECTIONS: Questions 18 through 22, inclusive, show standard symbols used on drawings. For each symbol, select the word or phrase which BEST describes the symbol.

18.

   A. Battery
   C. Open contact
   B. Capacitor
   D. Relay

19.

   A. Circuit breaker house
   C. Station platform
   B. Duct cross-section
   D. Street manhole

20.

   A. Messenger cable
   B. Single pole, double throw switch
   C. Earphones
   D. Circuit breaker

21.

   A. Auxiliary transformer
   C. Diode
   B. Emergency alarm
   D. Substation telephone

22.

   A. Cable splice
   C. Fuse
   B. Platform manhole
   D. Control terminal box

23. In a balanced, three-phase, four-wire wye-connected A.C. circuit, the

   A. phase voltage is equal to the line voltage
   B. line current is equal to the phase current
   C. line voltage is equal to twice the phase voltage
   D. current through the neutral is three times the phase current

4 (#2)

24. The identifying number F14 on a cable indicates the

   A. negative cable to zone 14
   B. supervisory cable to zone 14
   C. control cable to substation number 14
   D. battery cable to substation number 14

25. An overspeed device on a rotary converter having synchronous speed of 320 rpm is set to operate at 20% overspeed. The device will operate when the speed of the rotary reaches APPROXIMATELY _____ rpm.

   A. 255   B. 300   C. 340   D. 385

26. Each device used in the automatic switching equipment in the power department has been assigned a *device number*.
    The PRIMARY purpose of this numbering system is to

   A. make it more convenient when referring to blueprints
   B. simplify the ordering of replacement parts
   C. indicate the function of the device
   D. prevent confusion between rotary and rectifier equipment

27. The pilot cell of a substation control battery is that cell which

   A. is the middle cell for all batteries
   B. gives the lowest voltage reading on test
   C. gives the highest specific gravity reading on test
   D. is selected as the representative cell for the whole battery

28. In the power department, the voltage level used to differentiate between low voltage and high voltage apparatus is MOST NEARLY _____ volts.

   A. 440   B. 600   C. 700   D. 1000

29. The proper method of determining whether a hand carried carbon dioxide fire extinguisher is undercharged is to weigh it. This type of extinguisher is considered undercharged when the loss of weight is AT LEAST _____ of the charge weight.

   A. 10%   B. 25%   C. 50%   D. 75%

30. In performing a dielectric test of transformer insulating oil, you find, after making the required number of breakdowns on each filling, that the sample you are testing has a mean average breakdown value of 18KV.
    The NEXT step that should be taken is to

   A. notify the section office immediately
   B. take a second sample and test immediately
   C. restore all apparatus to normal operating positions
   D. increase the voltage applied to the sample at the rate of 3,000 volts per second

31. Of the following equipment located in automatic substations, scheduled maintenance is MOST frequently required on the

   A. anode circuit breaker
   B. M-G set
   C. battery panel
   D. rectifier water pump

32. The MAIN consideration which determines whether a protective relay should trip equipment immediately or merely sound an alarm is whether the fault in the equipment

   A. occurs at infrequent intervals
   B. is readily accessible for immediate repairs
   C. can be determined within a reasonable amount of time
   D. is dangerous to the point that it can cause permanent damage to the equipment

33. A rectifier cold seepage test

   A. has no relation to a bake-out in any way
   B. need be made only after a rectifier is baked out
   C. need be made only before a rectifier is baked out
   D. must be performed before a bake-out is started and after the bake-out is completed

34. If there is a discrepancy between the tag on a cable and duct assignment drawing, final positive identification of this cable is BEST made by

   A. spiking the cable
   B. using tracer current
   C. using a D.C. and an A.C. voltmeter
   D. cutting and splicing the cable

35. In the event of a failure to ground in certain substations, one of the purposes of the ground protection is to AUTOMATICALLY

   A. ground the negative bus
   B. de-energize the 600-volt bus
   C. switch the 600 volts D.C. to another substation
   D. switch the high tension feeders to the nearest substation

36. Two tests used to check a silicon diode are the _____ test and the _____ test.

   A. power dissipation; CFM
   B. calibration; surge current
   C. ohmmeter; peak reverse current
   D. thermal current rating; high voltage

37. The newly installed silicon rectifiers are 12-phase rather than single-phase or 3-phase rectifiers. One of the PRINCIPAL reasons for this is that

   A. less routine maintenance is required.
   B. the cathode carries a smaller current
   C. a smoother, more even D.C. voltage is obtained
   D. an even number of phases is essential for good operation

Questions 38-40.

DIRECTIONS: Questions 38 through 40, inclusive, refer to Column I and Column II below. For each method of putting rotary converters into service as listed in Column I, select the sentence in Column II which BEST applies to the particular method

COLUMN I

38. From the A.C. side

39. From the D.C. side

40. By means of special motors

COLUMN II

A. When starting, machine is fully separately excited and when machine is up to speed, shunt field connections are transferred to self-excitation

B. Induction motor is started at 58% of normal voltage supplied by auxiliary step-down transformers through an intervening 440-volt bus

C. Induction motor is coupled directly to rotary shaft and has one less pair of poles than converter

D. In starting, transformer primary is wye (star) connected and when rotary is up to normal speed, transformer connections are switched to delta

38.____
39.____
40.____

KEY (CORRECT ANSWERS)

1.	D	11.	A	21.	C	31.	D
2.	B	12.	B	22.	C	32.	D
3.	B	13.	D	23.	B	33.	D
4.	D	14.	B	24.	B	34.	B
5.	C	15.	A	25.	D	35.	B
6.	C	16.	D	26.	C	36.	C
7.	A	17.	C	27.	D	37.	C
8.	C	18.	A	28.	C	38.	D
9.	D	19.	B	29.	A	39.	A
10.	A	20.	D	30.	B	40.	C

EXAMINATION SECTION
TEST 1

DIRECTIONS: Each question or incomplete statement is followed by several suggested answers or completions. Select the one that BEST answers the question or completes the statement. *PRINT THE LETTER OF THE CORRECT ANSWER IN THE SPACE AT THE RIGHT.*

1. The PRIME reason for not replacing a blown fuse with another fuse having a higher rating is that the

    A. fuse will blow
    B. higher rating fuse will not fit properly
    C. designed purpose of the fuse would be lost
    D. circuit will have a higher power consumption

2. In the event of a failure to ground in a power substation, the purpose of the ground protection is to automatically

    A. ground the negative bus
    B. de-energize the 600 volt feeder
    C. de-energize all high tension feeders
    D. switch the 600 volts D.C. to another substation

3. Two common tests that are used to check a silicon diode are the _____ test and the _____ test.

    A. power dissipation; CFM
    B. calibration; surge current
    C. ohmmeter; peak reverse current
    D. thermal current rating; high voltage

4. With respect to proper safety precautions on electrical maintenance tools, it would be MOST correct to state that the tool insulation

    A. insures the safety of the user
    B. provides protection against abrasion only
    C. is of most value in a wet working area
    D. should be supplemented with a ground protection

5. The term *high dielectric strength* is normally associated with the characteristic of a

    A. transformer
    B. type of insulation
    C. cable
    D. switch

6. A neon-glow lamp is a convenience and compact device used for

    A. precision ammeter protection
    B. precision wattmeter protection
    C. determining if a power circuit is alive
    D. testing the time delay of remote relays

7. In order to start motors that require high starting currents and relatively low operating currents, the starting relay should have a

   A. time delay feature
   B. floating line coil
   C. snap action feature
   D. compensating feature

8. As a power maintainer, you think that an FMI procedure should be changed in order to improve personnel safety. The MOST desirable way to submit your idea to management is by

   A. submitting it through the Employee Suggestion Plan
   B. attending the next foremen's safety meeting
   C. writing directly to the division superintendent
   D. discussing it at the next union meeting

9. As a newly appointed maintainer, you are assigned to work with a more experienced maintainer who pays no attention to the safety rules.
The PROPER procedure would be for you to

   A. work with the maintainer but watch him very carefully
   B. ask your foreman if you could review this maintainer's safety record
   C. refuse to work with this maintainer and ask your foreman for another assignment
   D. tell the maintainer, before starting to work, that you would like him to adhere to the safety rules for his protection and yours

10. Electrical indicating instruments are USUALLY damped to prevent

    A. the needle from going off-scale
    B. the needle from reading down-scale
    C. excessive oscillation of the needle
    D. damage to the instruments if it is dropped

11. If a steel nut must stay tight under vibration, the MOST practical procedure would be to

    A. drill a hole in the nut
    B. use a self-locking nut
    C. weld the nut to the bolt
    D. stake the threads at the end of the bolt

12. A rule of the transit authority states that *employees are required to report defective equipment to their superiors, even when the maintenance of the particular piece of equipment is handled by another department.*
The purpose of this rule is to

    A. encourage alertness
    B. fix responsibility
    C. prevent accidents
    D. take advantage of manufacturer's guarantees

13. A good practical test to determine whether or not a wetted-down motor is sufficiently dried out is a(n) _____ test.

    A. flash-over
    B. high-voltage breakdown
    C. armature resistance
    D. insulation resistance

14. To smooth pitted contacts of a D.C. feeder breaker, you should use 14.____

    A. a fine file
    B. coarse sandpaper
    C. emery cloth
    D. steel wool

15. A single-phase A.C. potential of 240 volts is required for test purposes. A 600 volt A.C. 15.____
    source and two identical transformers with 300 volt primaries and 120 volt secondaries
    are available.
    The transformers should be connected with primaries in _____, secondaries in
    _____.

    A. series; series
    B. series; parallel
    C. parallel; series
    D. parallel; parallel

16. Your foreman gives you verbal directions on how to dismantle some equipment. After a 16.____
    period of time, you find that you cannot proceed with the dismantling in accordance with
    the procedure outlined by your foreman.
    Your BEST course of action is to

    A. use your own judgment
    B. ask your foreman for a further explanation
    C. discuss it with your helper
    D. discuss it with another maintainer

17. Before work is started on any power equipment, a Hold-Off tag MUST be 17.____

    A. in the System Operator's office
    B. attached to the piece of equipment to be worked on
    C. in the personal possession of the man in charge of the work
    D. attached to the control switch of the equipment to be worked on

18. A *trip-free,* manually operated air circuit breaker is one which 18.____

    A. does not open on sustained overloads
    B. does not open on instantaneous overloads
    C. has a defective mechanism and opens too readily
    D. can be opened by overloads while the closing handle is held in the closed position

19. Transit employees are cautioned not to use water to extinguish fires caused by high volt- 19.____
    age arcing.
    The MOST important reason for this rule is that the water

    A. may conduct the current and create a shock hazard
    B. will cause corrosion of sensitive electrical parts
    C. would cause the fuses to blow in electrical circuits
    D. coming into contact with an electrical arc releases asphyxiating fumes

20. When lifting very heavy objects, a maintainer should have assistance and 20.____

    A. lift using only his arm muscles
    B. lift using only his back muscles
    C. lean over the object to be lifted
    D. lift making full use of his leg muscles

21. If a co-worker is in contact with a high-voltage circuit, the FIRST action taken by you should be to

    A. call the doctor
    B. call the foreman
    C. cut off the power
    D. get the first aid kit

22. The MAIN purpose of the oil in an oil-filled power transformer is to

    A. quench arcing
    B. provide insulation
    C. prevent corrosion
    D. provide lubrication

23. In an A.C. circuit, the ratio of watts to voltamperes is to

    A. load factor
    B. power factor
    C. impedance
    D. efficiency

24. The MAXIMUM current that a circuit breaker can carry continuously is determined by its

    A. maximum trip setting
    B. instantaneous trip setting
    C. rated current capacity
    D. current interrupting capacity

25. An ammeter reads 6 amperes at full scale and has an internal resistance of 0.1 ohms. If this ammeter is to be used to register 60 amperes at full scale, it MUST be supplied with a shunt of _____ ohms.

    A. 0.011 B. 0.090 C. 0.900 D. 1.000

26. A transformer built so that both the primary and the secondary currents flow through the same winding is known as a(n) _____ transformer.

    A. auto-
    B. insulating
    C. variable-ratio
    D. constant-current

27. Of the following, the factor which determines the LARGEST capacity of fuse that may be used in a given circuit is the

    A. largest size of wire beyond the fuse
    B. minimum overload expected
    C. importance of maintaining the circuit alive
    D. number of fuses previously blown in the circuit

28. The secondary windings of energized current transformers are short circuited before opening the secondary circuit to

    A. clear the secondary circuit from ground
    B. maintain the continuity of the primary circuit
    C. prevent excessive current flow in the secondary winding
    D. prevent building up a high voltage in the secondary winding

29. Four resistors having respective current ratings of 2.5, 4, 4.5, and 6 amperes are connected in series.
    If the resistors are not to be overloaded, the MAXIMUM current permissible in this circuit is _____ amperes.

    A. 2.5 B. 4.25 C. 6 D. 17

30. The proper arrangement of the following wire sizes, in the order of increasing electrical resistance, is

   A. 2; 4/0; 1/0
   B. 1/0; 4/0; 2
   C. 2; 1/0; 4/0
   D. 4/0; 1/0; 2

31. Operating instructions are issued by the department

   A. for the guidance of employees
   B. for reading when the employee is not busy
   C. as a basis for evaluating employee performance
   D. to justify penalties in case of errors in operation

32. In a balanced, three-phase, three-wire, delta-connected circuit, the line voltages are equal

   A. to the phase voltages
   B. but the line currents are unequal
   C. but the phase voltages are unequal
   D. to three times the value of the sum of the phase voltages

Questions 33-39.

DIRECTIONS: Questions 33 through 39, inclusive, refer to the D.C. wiring diagram below. Unless otherwise stated, all switches are open. Neglect the effects of the ammeter and voltmeter on the circuit.

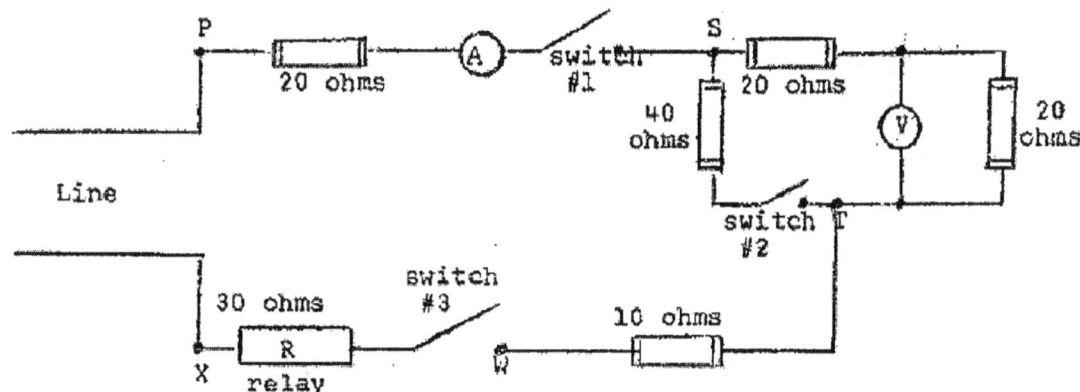

33. A circuit resistance of 100 ohms is obtained by closing switch nos.

   A. 1, 2, and 3
   B. 2 and 3
   C. 1 and 3
   D. 1 and 2

34. With all switches closed and 2 amperes flowing through the 40 ohm resistor, the line voltage is _____ volts.

   A. 80   B. 160   C. 240   D. 320

35. With all switches closed and the ammeter reading 1 ampere, the power consumed by the circuit is _____ watts.

   A. 60   B. 80   C. 100   D. 140

36. With switch nos. 1 and 3 closed and a line voltage of 100 volts D.C., the voltmeter reading should be _____ volts.   36. ____

   A. 0   B. 20   C. 40   D. 80

37. The relay (R) requires at least 1.10 amperes to operate. With a line voltage of 100 volts D.C., it will be operated by closing switch nos.   37. ____

   A. 1 and 2   B. 1 and 3
   C. 2 and 3   D. 1, 2, and 3

38. If the two lead wires to the ammeter are reversed, and all switches were closed, the   38. ____

   A. ammeter should indicate zero current
   B. ammeter needle should move backwards
   C. ammeter will continue to indicate properly
   D. current in the entire circuit will be reversed

39. With all switches closed, and a line voltage of 50 V D.C., the LARGEST voltage drop should be across points   39. ____

   A. P and S   B. S and T   C. T and W   D. W and X

40. Sediment found at the bottom of a lead-acid battery cell is MAINLY due to   40. ____

   A. the addition of water
   B. disintegration of the container
   C. precipitation from the electrolyte
   D. active material dropped from the plates

41. Good practice requires that cartridge fuses be removed from their clips with a fuse puller rather than with the bare hand to avoid   41. ____

   A. personal injury
   B. breaking the fuse
   C. damage to the fuse clips
   D. the possibility of drawing an arc

42. When preparing a new batch of electrolyte for a lead-acid battery, the acid should be poured into the water and not the water into the acid to avoid   42. ____

   A. dangerous splattering
   B. corrosion of the mixing vessel
   C. making the mixture too weak
   D. making the mixture too strong

43. Feed back from a control battery to the charging generator is USUALLY guarded against by   43. ____

   A. fuses in the battery charging circuit
   B. no-load protection on the charging set motor
   C. a low voltage trip on the generator circuit breaker
   D. a reverse current trip on the generator circuit breaker

44. When the control battery is *floated* on the bus of a motor-generator set, the generator is adjusted to

   A. share the constant control load equally, with the battery
   B. maintain constant line voltage regardless of the control demand
   C. stop when the battery is fully charged and start again when the battery voltage drops
   D. carry the constant load and also send a small current into the battery to keep it fully charged

45. The color of the prescribed Power Department NOT CLEAR tag is

   A. blue   B. green   C. red   D. yellow

46. On a certain voltmeter, the same scale is used for three ranges; these are 0-750, 0-300, and 0-15 volts.
   If the scale is marked only for the 0-750 volt range, a scale reading of 150 when the 300-volt range is being used corresponds to an actual voltage of _____ volts.

   A. 15   B. 60   C. 150   D. 350

47. As soon as a test potential has been removed from a piece of high voltage equipment,

   A. all safety grounds can be removed
   B. the person in charge should survey the area and remove the high voltage caution sign
   C. the equipment should be discharged to ground before anyone is allowed to come in contact with it
   D. the person in charge shall immediately inform the employee in charge of the apparatus that the test is over

48. The SMALLEST number of single-phase A.C. wattmeters required to measure the power in a three-phase, 4-wire, unbalanced delta-wye connected A.C. circuit is

   A. 4   B. 3   C. 2   D. 1

49. Before repairing an electric power tool, the preferred safety practice is to

   A. remove the power to the tool
   B. ground both sides of the power supply
   C. stand on an insulated mat
   D. place the tool on an insulated mat

50. In electrical work, the symbol Hz indicates

   A. watts per hour   B. cycles per second
   C. very high voltage   D. horsepower rating

51. The BEST immediate first aid if electrolyte splashes into the eyes when filling a storage battery is to

   A. bandage the eyes to keep out light
   B. wipe the eyes dry with a soft towel
   C. bathe the eyes with plenty of clean water
   D. induce tears to flow by staring at a bright light

52. The electrical power for each section of the subway signal system is arranged to come from either one of two supply feeders.
The MOST likely reason for this arrangement is to

   A. avoid the use of very large cables
   B. divide the load between two power plants
   C. keep the supply voltage as low as possible
   D. provide continuing service if one feeder goes dead

53. Assume a fellow employee has lost his pass and asks you to lend him your pass to be used to perform an errand for the foreman.
You should

   A. lend the pass if the foreman approves
   B. refuse because you might need the pass yourself
   C. refuse because the pass is issued for your own use only
   D. lend the pass because it is going to be used on a legitimate errand

54. In the power department, the voltage level used to differentiate between low voltage and high voltage apparatus is MOST NEARLY _____ volts.

   A. 440   B. 600   C. 750   D. 1000

55. Tools which are damaged should

   A. be used only for unimportant work
   B. be used until replacements can be obtained
   C. not be used because personal injury might result
   D. not be used because you may be held responsible for the damage

56. The BEST time to adjust the brushes on a D.C. motor is when the motor is

   A. de-energized
   B. running at no load
   C. running at full load
   D. operated as a generator with a test bank of lamps

57. You will probably be MOST highly regarded by your superiors if you show that you

   A. like your work by asking all the questions you can about it
   B. are interested in improving the job by continually offering suggestions
   C. are willing to do your share by completing assigned tasks properly and on time
   D. are on the job by volunteering information whenever you think someone has violated a safety rule

58. In standard report forms, it is advisable to print rather than write in the entries because printing generally

   A. looks better   B. is more legible
   C. occupies less space   D. is easier to do

59. The sum of 1 9/16", 3 1/2", 7 3/8", 10 3/4", and 12 5/8" is

   A. 33 11/16"   B. 34 13/16"
   C. 35 11/16"   D. 35 13/16"

60. A rule of the transit authority states that *Employees must be thoroughly acquainted with, and qualified to operate, all equipment which they may be required to handle in the performance of their duties.*
    The probable reason for this rule is that

    A. an employee should be able to perform his duties properly
    B. all employees must be able to operate all transit equipment
    C. an employee can be kept busy operating equipment during a slow period
    D. an employee should be able to substitute for a higher titled employee at any time

---

KEY (CORRECT ANSWERS)

1. C	16. B	31. A	46. B
2. B	17. D	32. A	47. C
3. C	18. D	33. C	48. B
4. D	19. A	34. D	49. A
5. B	20. D	35. B	50. B
6. C	21. C	36. B	51. C
7. A	22. B	37. D	52. D
8. A	23. B	38. B	53. C
9. D	24. C	39. D	54. C
10. C	25. A	40. D	55. C
11. B	26. A	41. A	56. A
12. C	27. B	42. A	57. C
13. D	28. D	43. D	58. B
14. A	29. A	44. D	59. D
15. A	30. D	45. D	60. A

TEST 2

DIRECTIONS: Each question or incomplete statement is followed by several suggested answers or completions. Select the one that BEST answers the question or completes the statement. *PRINT THE LETTER OF THE CORRECT ANSWER IN THE SPACE AT THE RIGHT.*

1. The section of a mercury arc rectifier which maintains low pressure in the vacuum tank is the _____ system. 1._____

   A. pumping   B. ignition   C. excitation   D. cooling

2. The local emergency control key and lamp group located in the control room consists of a green lamp, a red lamp, a control key, a(n) 2._____

   A. select key, and an operate key
   B. white lamp, and a select key
   C. amber lamp, and a white lamp
   D. indication key, and an operate key

3. During a bakeout, of a mercury arc rectifier, a voltmeter is connected between the tank and cathode to detect arcing.
   The PROPER voltmeter to use should have a range of 0 - _____ volts _____. 3._____

   A. 30; D.C.   B. 60; D.C.   C. 150; A.C.   D. 300; A.C.

4. The purpose of the glob tube in a telemetering circuit is to provide protection should the _____ become _____. 4._____

   A. line wires; open-circuited
   B. line wires; short-circuited
   C. disc film cut-out; inoperative
   D. filament transformer; short-circuited

5. While a certain zone is being operated from the local emergency control panel in the control room, a rectifier trips off the line automatically.
   The indication obtained in the control room is a change in indicating lights from red to green and 5._____

   A. a bell signal
   B. a white light
   C. no other indication
   D. a bell signal and a white light

6. Low tension A.C. power is furnished to the substations for auxiliary equipment at 6._____

   A. 110 volts, single-phase
   B. 600 volts, single-phase
   C. 220 volts, 2-phase, 4-wire
   D. 208/120 volts, 3-phase, 4-wire

7. A common feature of devices 23R, 26H, 26L, and 26R is that ALL are actuated by 7._____

   A. current   B. pressure   C. temperature   D. voltage

8. When drawing a sample of insulating oil for test from an oil circuit breaker having a sampling cock, about two quarts of oil should be drained out before taking a sample.
This is done

   A. to agitate the oil in the tank before sampling
   B. because the first two quarts always have water present
   C. to obtain sufficient oil to rinse out the sample bottle
   D. so that the sample represents the oil in the tank and not that in the drain pipe

9. A mercury arc rectifier is usually equipped with both a mercury vacuum pump and a rotary vacuum pump.
The reason for having two pumps is that the

   A. mercury pump is not suited for continuous operation
   B. rotary pump alone cannot produce the required degree of vacuum
   C. rotary pump serves as a reserve unit in case of failure of the mercury pump
   D. mercury pump serves as a reserve unit in case of failure of the rotary pump

10. The newly installed silicon rectifiers in the NYCTA are 12-phase rather than single-phase or 3-phase rectifiers.
One of the PRINCIPAL reasons for this is that

   A. less routine maintenance is required
   B. the cathode carries a smaller current
   C. a smoother, more even D.C. voltage is obtained
   D. an even number of phases is essential for good operation

11. Each device used in the automatic switching equipment in the power department has been assigned a *device number*. The PRIMARY purpose of the particular numbering system used is

   A. for convenience when referring to blueprints
   B. to simplify the ordering of replacement parts
   C. to indicate the function of the particular device
   D. to identify the location of the device in the substation

12. The position of all supervised units may be checked at the System Operation board at any time by pushing the _____ key.

   A. control   B. operate   C. select   D. start

13. A bake-out is GENERALLY considered necessary for a rectifier if

   A. it has been subjected to a heavy overload
   B. it has been open to the atmosphere for a long period
   C. it has been operating at light load for a long period
   D. more than three months have elapsed since a previous bake-out

14. The relief diaphragm is installed on a rectifier power transformer to provide protection agains

   A. excessive voltage   B. excessive oil pressure
   C. high vacuum   D. high water pressure

15. When a rectifier is *held off* and disconnected from the station positive bus, the power connections to the inter-phase transformer should

    A. be connected to ground
    B. never be grounded
    C. all be tied to the negative bus
    D. be tied to the positive side of a low potential safety relay

16. In a rectifier cooling system, a section of rubber hose is used on each side of the

    A. water pump, for flexibility
    B. heat exchanger, for heat insulation
    C. surge tank, for ease of connection
    D. rectifier tank, for electrical insulation

17. The purpose of device 49A on the battery charging MG set is to

    A. adjust voltage
    B. protect the motor against overload
    C. connect the motor to the supply lines
    D. connect the generator to the control bus

18. The neutral of the interphase transformer is connected to the

    A. D.C. negative bus
    B. substation ground
    C. power transformer neutral
    D. D.C. positive bus

19. A rectifier is given a seepage test in order to determine

    A. the tightness of tank and pipe line
    B. if its cooling coils are tight
    C. the condition and amount of mercury in the chamber
    D. if the heating coils are functioning properly

20. The identifying number F14 on a cable would indicate the

    A. negative cable to zone 14
    B. supervisory cable to zone 14
    C. control cable to substation number 14
    D. battery cable to substation number 14

KEY (CORRECT ANSWERS)

1. A
2. D
3. B
4. A
5. C

6. D
7. C
8. D
9. B
10. C

11. C
12. D
13. B
14. B
15. B

16. D
17. B
18. A
19. A
20. B

TEST 3

DIRECTIONS: Each question or incomplete statement is followed by several suggested answers or completions. Select the one that BEST answers the question or completes the statement. *PRINT THE LETTER OF THE CORRECT ANSWER IN THE SPACE AT THE RIGHT.*

1. An overspeed device on a rotary converter having synchronous speed of 280 rpm is set to operate at 15% overspeed. It will operate when the speed of the rotary reaches about _____ rpm.
   A. 240 B. 295 C. 320 D. 360

   1._____

2. On receiving an emergency alarm at a substation, after noting the code signal and the time, the NEXT thing the substation operator should do is

   A. notify system operation office
   B. restore the *drop* switch to its *up* position
   C. check that all breakers have opened that should have opened

   2._____

3. One purpose of the milliammeter on the emergency alarm panel in a substation is to

   A. indicate when all tracks are de-energized
   B. provide a check on the gong code signal
   C. measure the tripping current for the feeder breakers
   D. give an indication that the subway circuit is closed

   3._____

4. When cleaning a rotary converter, it is MOST correct to

   A. carefully wipe the A.C. and D.C. brushes with a rag
   B. carefully blow down the A.C. and D.C. brushes with compressed air
   C. lift the brushes from the brush boxes and wipe the contact surfaces
   D. carefully clean the A.C. and D.C. brush holders with a vacuum cleaner

   4._____

5. When shutting down a rotary converter, it is common practice to adjust the power factor to unity

   A. *before* opening the oil circuit breaker
   B. *before* opening the positive switch
   C. *after* opening the equalizer breaker or switch
   D. *after* opening the battery switch on the rotary converter panel

   5._____

6. A rotary converter is used to

   A. change A.C. power into D.C. power
   B. step-down the substation against abnormal conditions
   C. protect the substation against abnormal conditions
   D. equalize the A.C. power input with the D.C. power output

   6._____

7. The pilot cell of a substation control battery is that cell which

   A. is the middle cell for all batteries
   B. gives the lowest voltage reading on test
   C. gives the highest specific gravity reading on test
   D. is selected as the representative cell for the whole battery

   7._____

8. The difference between the JR36 breaker, when used as device 72 rather than device 54, is that as device 72 the breaker

   A. is trip-free
   B. has a lower voltage rating
   C. has a lower amperage rating
   D. has inductive shunts and a bucking bar

9. When a rotary converter is started as a D.C. motor, it is brought up to speed

   A. with its shunt field separate excited
   B. shunt field of self-excited
   C. with the use of a field reversing switch
   D. without the use of any starting resistance

10. A device used in some substations to convert A.C. to D.C. for starting purposes is called a(n)

    A. equalizer
    B. motor-generator set
    C. field transfer switch
    D. rotary power transformer

11. When starting a rotary converter by means of an induction motor, the induction motor

    A. is adjusted so that its synchronous speed is less than the rotary speed
    B. is mounted on the shaft of the rotary and has two less poles than the rotary
    C. has its speed controlled for synchronization by adjusting the A.C. voltage to the motor
    D. affects the rotary power factor by a change in the induction motor's shunt field excitation

12. The PRINCIPAL use of the main blowers in a substation is to

    A. cool the transformers
    B. ventilate the station
    C. cool the rotary converters
    D. provide compressed air to blow out the rotaries

13. The particular rotary to be used under light-load conditions is usually varied from time to time in a multi-unit station.
    The BEST reason for doing this is so that

    A. the power factor can be kept uniform
    B. all the rotaries receive about the same wear
    C. the operator can become experienced on all the rotaries
    D. the rotary performances can be compared with one another

14. The nominal speed of a rotary converter is governed by the

    A. A.C. voltage and D.C. load
    B. D.C. load and the shunt field current
    C. excitation of the shunt field and the A.C. voltage
    D. frequency of the A.C. supply and the number of poles

15. A rotary, started as a D.C. motor, is brought into synchronism by adjusting the   15.____

    A. D.C. bus voltage   B. rotary power factor
    C. shunt field current   D. A.C. supply frequency

16. When a rotary converter is started from the A.C. side, all the D.C. brushes are usually   16.____
    raised from the commutator except for one positive and one negative brush. These two
    brushes are left in contact with the commutator to

    A. permit speed control
    B. provide relay protection
    C. indicate the D.C. polarity
    D. maintain unity power factor

17. When a rotary converter is being synchronized, the oil circuit breaker control switch   17.____
    should be closed at the instant the synchroscope pointer

    A. points horizontally to the left
    B. points horizontally to the right
    C. reaches the vertically upward position
    D. reaches the vertically downward position

18. When shutting down a rotary converter during light load hours, the FIRST thing you   18.____
    should do after reducing the load is to

    A. trip the positive breaker
    B. open the oil circuit breaker
    C. open the battery switch
    D. close the transformer dampers

19. When dielectric tests indicate the presence of water in transformer oil, the water is USU-   19.____
    ALLY removed by having the oil

    A. boiled   B. distilled
    C. filtered   D. chemically treated

20. Rotary converters are NEVER started   20.____

    A. as synchronous motors
    B. from the D.C. bus as shunt motors
    C. by a direct connected induction motor
    D. as series motors from the D.C. bus

KEY (CORRECT ANSWERS)

1.	C	11.	B
2.	C	12.	A
3.	D	13.	B
4.	B	14.	D
5.	A	15.	C
6.	A	16.	C
7.	D	17.	C
8.	D	18.	A
9.	A	19.	C
10.	B	20.	D

BASIC FUNDAMENTALS OF BRIDGES IN ELECTRICAL MEASUREMENT

CONTENTS

		Page
1.	INTRODUCTION	1
2.	WHEATSTONE BRIDGE	1
3.	MEASURING CAPACITANCE WITH A BRIDGE	2
4.	MEASURING INDUCTANCE WITH A BRIDGE	4
5.	PRACTICAL IMPEDANCE BRIDGE	5
6.	SUMMARY	7
7.	REVIEW QUESTIONS	9

BASIC FUNDAMENTALS OF BRIDGES IN ELECTRICAL MEASUREMENT

1. Introduction

A bridge is a sensitive device used to measure resistance, capacitance, or inductance when great accuracy of measurement is desired. The bridges can be used also for measuring reactance, impedance, and frequency. All bridge circuits include a source of a-c or d-c voltage; an indicating device, usually a sensitive galvanometer or headphones; an adjustable standard, usually a resistor or capacitor; the unknown whose value is to be measured; and a method of determining how much the un- known value differs from the standard.

2. Wheatstone Bridge

a. The most common type of bridge used is the *Wheatstone* bridge (fig. 00). The bridge shown is known as the *diamond* arrangement, because the four resistors are shown schematically in the form of a diamond. Resistor R_x is the unknown resistor, R_a and R_b are known as *ratio arms,* and R_s as the *standard arm* of the bridge. R_a and R_b are fixed resistors in the bridge that provide a specific ratio of R_a/R_b, and maximum accuracy and sensitivity result when this ratio is 1/1. With the unknown resistor, R_x, inserted in the bridge, rheostat R_s is adjusted until the galvanometer reads zero. When this occurs, the voltage drops across R_a and R_b equal the voltage drops across Rs and R_x. In A, where R_a equals R_b, the ohmic value of R_s (450 ohms) must equal that of R_x for this condition to exist.

b. In B, a slightly different condition exists and the ratio of R_a/R_b is made equal to 200/600 or 1/3. To balance the bridge so that the galvanometer reads zero, the ratio of R_s/R_x must also be 1/3. Since R_s equals 150 ohms, then R_x must equal 450 ohms. This line of reasoning, when put in mathematical form, is shown by the formula,

$$\frac{R_a}{R_b} = \frac{R_s}{R_x}$$

Transposing this equation,

$$R_x = \frac{R_s \times R_b}{R_a} = \frac{150 \times 600}{200} = 450 \text{ ohms.}$$

c. Another Wheatstone bridge circuit, known as a slide-wire bridge, is shown in figure 01. A slide wire, made of a material such as man-ganin and consisting of a single wire divided in 100 equal parts, forms the ratio arm of the bridge. A contact point that can be moved manually along the wire is provided; the re-

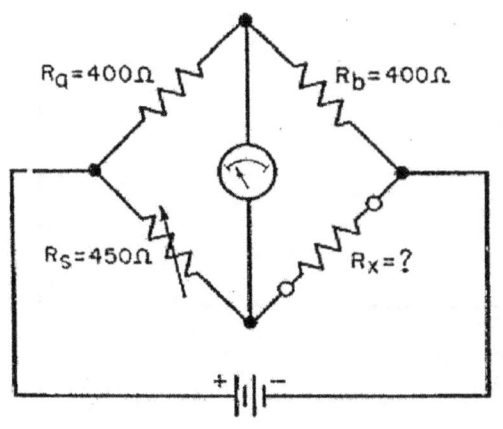 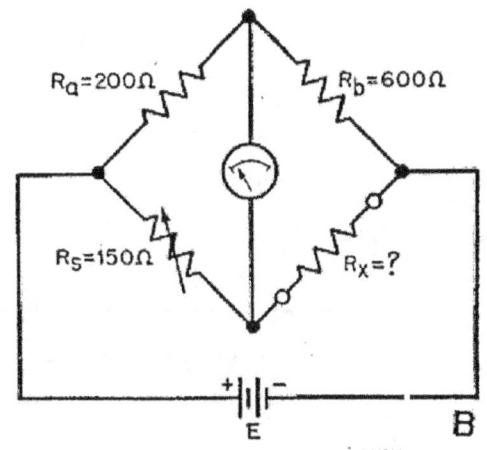

Figure 00. *Determining an unknown resistance using diamond arrangement of Wheatstone bridge.*

sistance to the left of the contact point represents R_a and that to the right represents resistor R_b. Moving the manually operated contact point along the slide wire varies the R_a/R_b ratio. The standard resistor, R_s, has four steps of 1, 10, 100, or 1,000 ohms, making it possible for the bridge to measure different ranges of resistance. An example of the method used to find the value of an unknown resistor can be shown by setting selector switch S to place 10 ohms in the arm. With the contact point in the position shown, scale A gives the value of R_a as 40 ohms, and scale B gives the value of R_b or 60 ohms. The unknown resistor, R_x, then can be found by the formula

$$R_x = \frac{R_s \times R_b}{R_a} = \frac{10 \times 60}{40} = 15 \text{ ohms}$$

Nonuniformity of the resistance of the slide wire makes this type of bridge less accurate than the diamond arrangement.

3. Measuring Capacitance with a Bridge

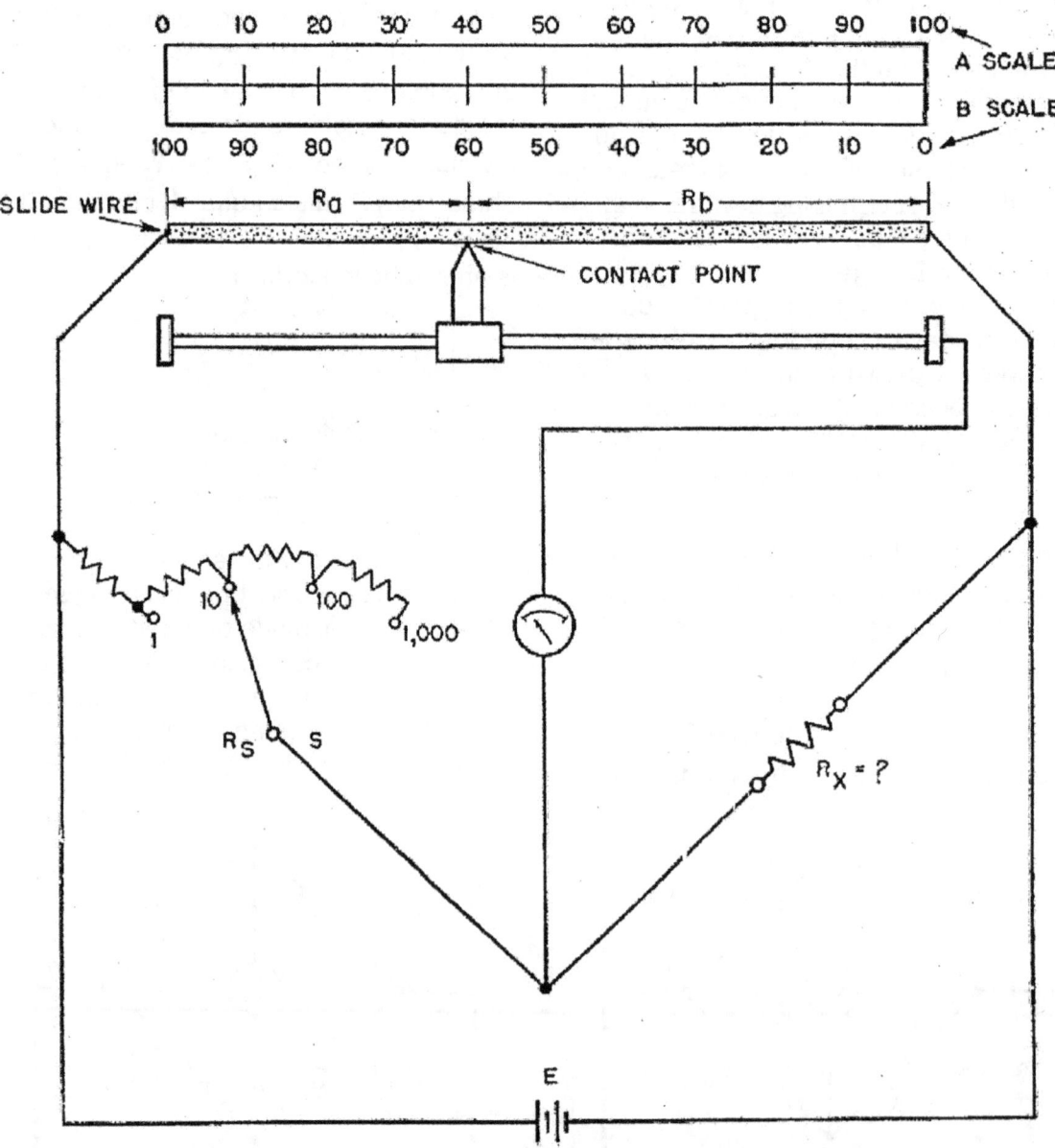

Figure 01. Determining an unknown resistance using slide-wire bridge.

a. When measuring an unknown capacitance on a bridge, an a-c source of voltage must be used. This is necessary because the reactance of the unknown capacitor is used to determine its capacitive value. Some typical methods of determining an unknown capacitance are given in figure 102. In the *series-resistance* capacitive bridge, in A, an a-c generator replaces the battery used in resistance measurements. Headphones are used as null indicators instead of a galvanometer, since their pickup response is dependent on the reactance presented by the unknown capacitance. The ratio arms consist of R_a and R_b, with R_a adjustable so that the R_a/R_b ratio can be varied. In the standard arm, a calibrated variable capacitor, C_s, is in series with an adjustable resistor R_s. Capacitor C_x is the unknown capacitance, and *Rex* represents the leakage resistance of the capacitor. When the bridge is balanced, the voltage drops across R^a, C_s, and R_s equal those across R_b, C_x, and R_{cx}. R_a is adjusted to give a specific R_a/R_b ratio, R_s is adjusted to compensate for the effects of R_{cx}, and C_s is adjusted to equal C_x. R_s and C_s are varied alternately until a zero beat is obtained in the headphones. The dial setting of C_s represents the unknown capacitance. The unknown capacitance can be computed mathematically by the relationship

$$C_x = C_s \times \frac{R_a}{R_b}.$$

6. Another method of determining the unknown capacitance, C_x, is illustrated in B. This is known as the *Schering* type of capacitance bridge. The distinguishing feature of this bridge is that the leakage resistance, R_{cx}, of the unknown capacitor is compensated for by the adjustable capacitor, C_a, which is in parallel with R_a. The fixed ratio arm, R_a, and the adjustable ratio arm, R_b, are connected across the headphones. C_a and the standard calibrated capacitor, C_s, are tuned until a zero beat is obtained in the headphones.

c. The capacitance of *electrolytic* capacitors, also, can be determined by using a capacitance bridge. However, a polarizing voltage supplied by a battery must be applied to the electrolytic capacitor, as shown in C. Capacitor C_r must be large enough that its reactance at the frequency of the a-c generator is a minimum so that the a-c voltage will be bypassed around the battery. The operation of this type of bridge arrangement is the same as the operation of other types of capacitance bridges.

d. When an unknown capacitance is small in value and great accuracy is desired, a *substitution* method is used commonly to determine its value. In this method, the resistors comprising the two ratio arms are made equal in value, and a known capacitor is connected across the terminals that are used to measure the unknown capacitor. The bridge then is balanced by adjusting the standard capacitor, and the reading of the dial setting is noted. The unknown capacitor is connected in parallel with the known capacitor, and the bridge is balanced once more by adjusting the standard capacitor. The

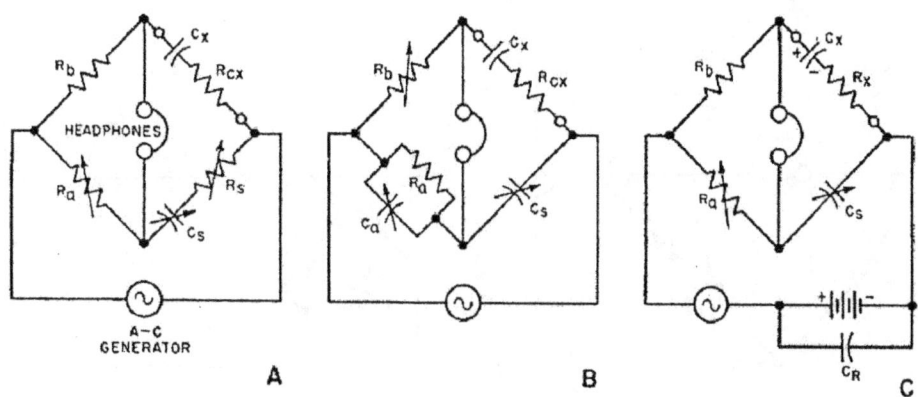

Figure 02. Typical bridge circuits for determining an unknown capacitance.

new reading of the dial setting is noted. The *difference* in the two readings is equal to the capacitance of the unknown.

e. The dissipation factor is the ratio of the resistance of a capacitor to its reactance and is a direct check of the capacitors quality. It is equal to

$$D=\frac{R_{cx}}{X_{cx}}, \text{ or } R_{cx} \times 2\pi fc_x$$

where D is the dissipation factor, R_{cx} is the leakage resistance, and X_{cx} the capacitive reactance of the capacitor. The greater the leakage resistance, the greater the dissipation factor, and when the capacitor has a higher dissipation factor than the value specified by the manufacturer, the capacitor should be discarded. In many capacitance bridges, provisions are made to measure the *dissipation, factor* of a capacitor, and many equipments have dials on which it is indicated directly.

4. Measuring Inductance with a Bridge

a. An unknown inductance can be determined by using the Maxwell bridge shown in A of figure 03. R_a and Rb are the ratio arms, and both are adjustable to obtain various R_a/R_b ratios. I_x represents the unknown inductance and R_x the resistance of the inductor. The standard resistance, R_s, is adjusted to cancel the effects of R_x, the standard inductance, and Ls is adjusted to balance the bridge and obtain zero beat in the headphones. The inductance of L_s as read on a calibrated dial equals that of the unknown inductance. The unknown inductance also can be computed by the relationship

$$L_x = \frac{L_s \times R_b}{R_s}.$$

b. Since it is difficult to calibrate accurately a standard variable inductor, variable capacitors often are used as the standard instead of inductors. One type of bridge using a capacitor as its standard (B, fig. 103) is a variation of the Maxwell bridge. The standard capacitor, C_s, is adjusted to obtain the proper voltage drops around the circuit, and Rs is adjusted to cancel the effects of R_x. The ratio arms, R_a and R_b, are used to help balance the bridge and are connected to opposite sides of L_x. Dials on the equipment are read to determine directly the inductive value of L_x in henrys, millihenrys, or microhenrys. Inductance also can be directly computed from the relationship

$$L_x = C_s \times R_a \times R_b.$$

c. Another bridge used for inductance meas- urements, known as an Owen bridge, is shown in A of figure 04. As in the Maxwell bridge, L_x is located opposite the standard capacitor, C_s, so that a comparison can be made between C_s and L_x. A fixed capacitor or a series of capacitors which are switched into the arm, one at a time, can be used to replace C_s. The variable capacitor, C_a, is used to balance out R_x, and R_a. and Rb balance the bridge. The mathematical relationship used for determining the unknown

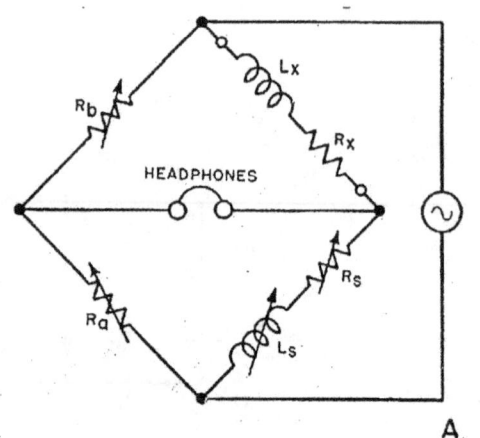
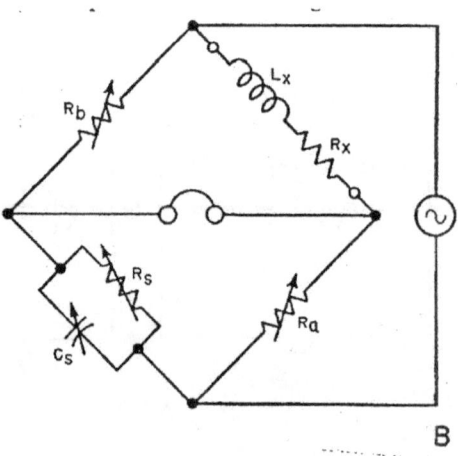

Figure 03. Methods for determining an unknown inductance, using a bridge circuit.

inductance in the Owen bridge is identical to that of the Maxwell bridge. Figure 04 shows the similarity between the Hay bridge and the Owen bridge. The standard capacitor, C_s, located opposite the unknown inductance, L_x, is in series with R_s. Rx is balanced by R_s, L_x is balanced by C_s, and the variable resistors, Ra and R_b, complete the balance of the bridge. This type generally is used for measuring inductances having a $Q(X_L/R)$ greater than 10.

d. Just as the dissipation factor is used to measure the quality of a capacitor, *storage factor* sometimes is used to measure the quality of an inductor. Storage factor is defined as the reciprocal of the dissipation factor and is equal to

$$S = \frac{X_L}{R_L}$$

where X_L is the inductive reactance of the coil and R_L the resistance of the inductor. This is identical to the Q (figure of merit) of a coil and it is desirable for an inductance to have a, high storage factor.

5. Practical Impedance Bridge
a. SCHEMATIC DIAGRAM.
1. The schematic of a practical impedance bridge used to measure resistance, capacitance, inductance, dissipation factor and storage factor is shown in figure 05. When measuring resistance, the unknown resistor is connected to the RES terminals. When measuring inductance or capacitance, the unknown reactor is connected to the L-C terminals. Switches S_2 *and* S_3 are ganged and when positioned as shown (R position), resistance can be measured. Switch S_1 determines the amount of resistance in the ratio arms. The resistors of S_1–A represent R_a and those of S_1_B represent R_b as used in previous bridge explanations.
2. With S_2 and S_3 in the C position, inductance, dissipation factor, and storage factor can be measured. The L-C terminals are connected, and the RES terminal is disconnected from the bridge. The lower sections of S_2 and S_3 connect positions, D, DQ, and Q. When in the D position, the upper sections of S_2 and S_3 are in the C position and the dissipation factor can be measured. The DQ position is used when it is desired to measure storage factor where the Q of the coil is less than 10, and the Q position is used for values of Q greater than 10. When measuring capacitance or dissipation factor, R_{11}, R_{13} and C_1 are included in the bridge circuit. R_{11} and R_{13} help balance the bridge, and C_1 is a d-c blocking capacitor. When measuring inductance or storage factor, R_{11}, R_{12}, and C_2 are included in the bridge circuit. R_{11} is used to balance the bridge for a storage factor greater than 10,

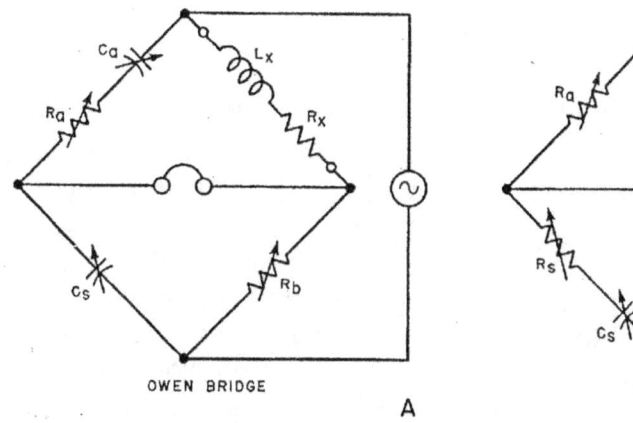

OWEN BRIDGE A   HAY BRIDGE B

Figure 04. Owen and Hay bridges used for determining an unknown inductance.

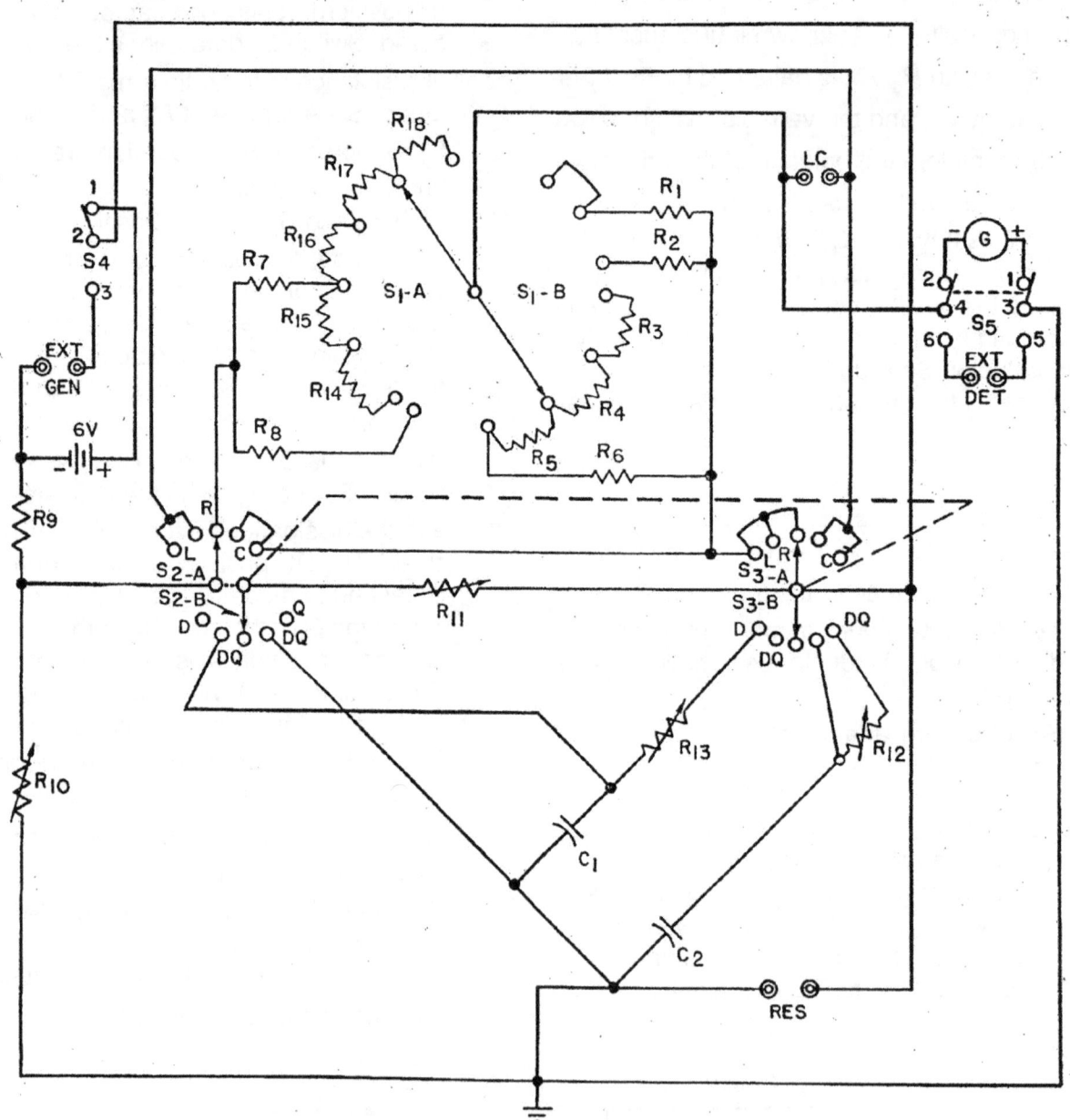

Figure 05. Schematic of typical practical impedance bridge.

and R_{12} for a storage factor less than 10. C_2 is a d-c blocking capacitor.

3. When resistance is being measured, switch S_5 is in the position shown, and the galvanometer is in the bridge circuit. When S_5 is in positions 5 and 6, headphones can be connected to the EXT DET terminals of the bridge circuit. S_5 remains in this position when measuring inductance or capacitance. When measuring resistance, with S_4 in the position shown, a 6-volt battery is inserted in the bridge circuit. When S_4 is thrown so that the EXT GEN terminals are connected to the bridge instead of the battery, an external a-c source, usually an audio oscillator, can be connected to the bridge. This is the position in which inductance and capacitance are measured. Resistor $R9$ is a current-limiting resistor for the external a-c generator.

b. CIRCUIT FOR MEASURING RESISTANCE. If the circuit of figure 05 is used to measure resistance, the conditions shown in the simplified diagram (fig. .06) exist. With switches S_2 and S_3 in the R positions and S_1–A as shown, the R_a ratio arm consists of R_7, R_{16}, and R_{17}. Switch S_1–B puts R_5 and R_6 in the ratio arm R_b. With S_5 in the position shown, the galvanometer also is in the bridge and the 6-volt battery is connected in the circuit. The unknown resistor, R_x, is inserted between the RES terminals, and the calibrated resistor, R_{10} (the standard) is adjusted to balance the bridge. The ohmic value of the unknown resistor is read on the panel of the bridge equipment. Its reading is dependent upon the ohmic values of the two ratio arms and R_{10}.

c. MAXWELL BRIDGE. The Maxwell bridge circuit arrangement of figure 05 can be used also to measure inductance and storage factor (fig. 07). With S_2 and S_3 in the L, DQ positions, headphones are connected to the EXT DET terminals, and an audio oscillator is connected to the EXT GEN terminals. The unknown inductor, L_x, then is connected to the L-C terminals and R_{10} and R_{11} are adjusted to balance the bridge (minimum indication in the headphones). Resistor R_x represents the d-c resistance of the unknown inductor. Inductance and storage factor are read directly from dials on the bridge equipment.

d. HAY BRIDGE. The circuit shown in figure 105 can be connected as a Hay bridge to measure inductance and storage factor (fig..08). The Hay bridge is used to measure storage factors greater than 10. The arrangement of all the switches in the Hay bridge is the same as those for the Maxwell bridge with the exception of S_2 and S_3. These switches are arranged so that their lower sections are connected to the Q position, their upper sections remaining in the L position. Resistor R_{12} in series with capacitor C_1 is the standard arm of the bridge. The remainder of the Hay bridge is identical to the Maxwell bridge arrangement.

e. CIRCUIT FOR MEASURING CAPACITANCE. The circuit of figure 05 also can be arranged (fig. 09) to measure an unknown capacitor and dissipation factor. Switches S_2 and S_3 are arranged so that their upper sections are in the C position and their lower sections are in the D position. This causes C_1 to be in series with R_{13} in the standard arm. R_5 and R_6 become the R_b ratio arm. C_x represents the capacitance to be measured, and R_x the d-c resistance of the capacitor. The bridge is balanced by adjusting R_{10} and R_{13}. A minimum indication is heard in the headphones, and capacitance, or dissipation factor, is read directly on the panel of the bridge.

6. Summary

a. A bridge is a sensitive device which is used to measure an unknown resistance, capacitance, inductance, or reactance.

b. The most common bridge used to measure an unknown resistance is the Wheatstone bridge.

c. The mathematical relationship for determining an unknown resistance in a bridge circuit is

$$R_x = \frac{R_s \times R_b}{R_a}.$$

d. A slide-wire Wheatstone bridge uses a single piece of high-resistance wire as the R_a and R_b ratio arms.

e. When measuring an unknown capacitance, an a-c generator and headphones are used instead of a battery and galvanometer as in a Wheatstone bridge.

f. The mathematical relationship for determining an unknown capacitor in a bridge circuit is

$$C_x = C_s \times \frac{R_a}{R_b}.$$

g. Dissipation factor determines the leakage resistance of a capacitor and is equal to the leakage resistance divided by the reactance of the capacitor, or $R_{cx} \times 2\pi f c_x$

h. Inductance bridges often use variable capacitors instead of variable inductors as the standard because they are easier to calibrate.

i. The mathematical relationship for determining an unknown inductor in a bridge circuit is

$$L_x = C_s \times R_a \times R_b.$$

j. Storage factor determines the worth of an inductor and is equal to its reactance divided by its d-c resistance.

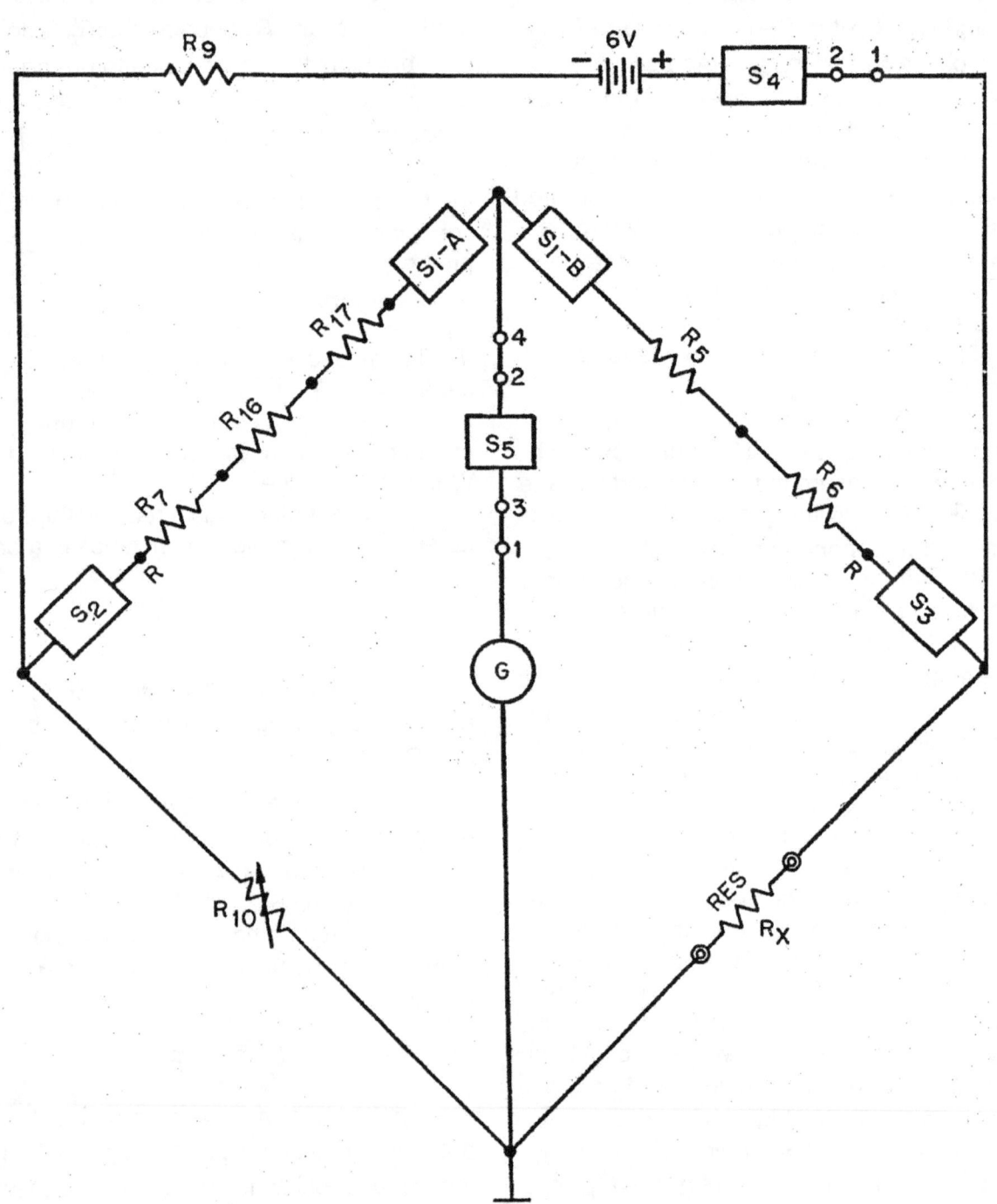

Figure 06. Circuit for measuring resistance.

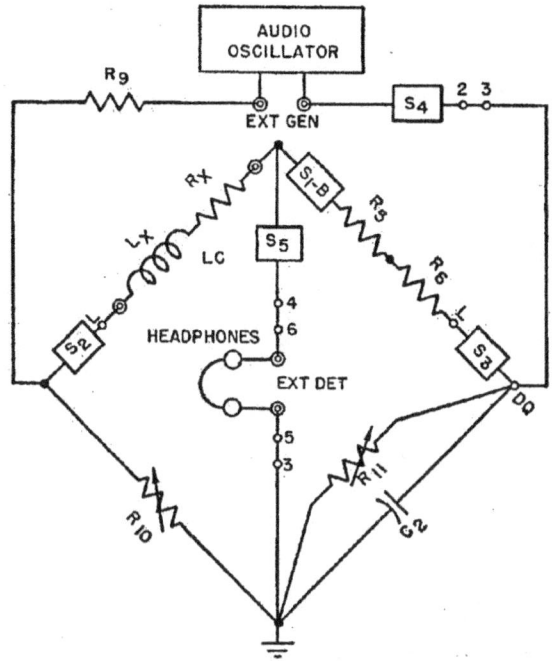

Figure 07. Maxwell bridge circuit for measuring inductance and storage factor.

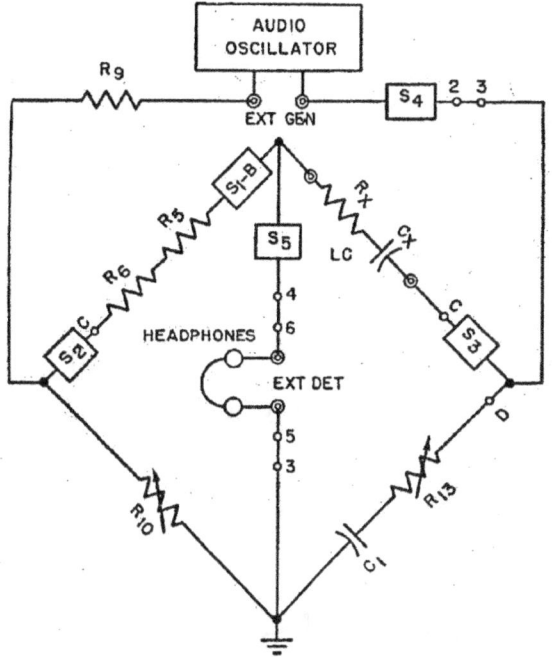

Figure 09. Circuit for measuring capacitance and dissipation factor.

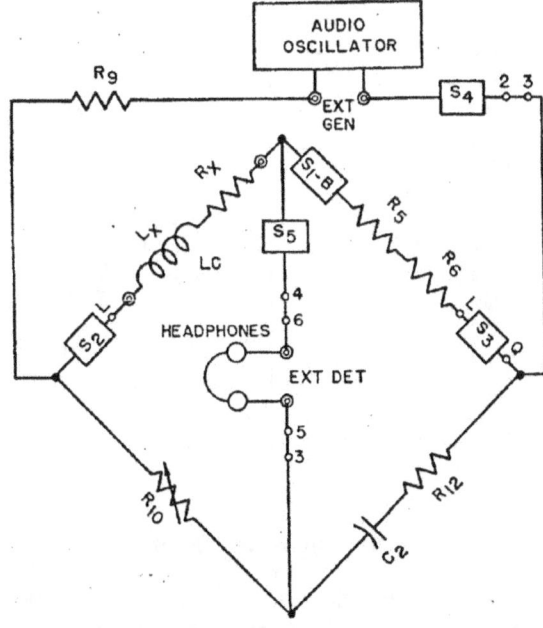

Figure 08. Hay bridge circuit for measuring inductance and storage factor.

7. Review Questions

a. Define a bridge circuit.

b. Can a Wheatstone bridge be used to measure an unknown reactance?

c. Why is it desirable to have the R_b/R_a ratio in a Wheatstone bridge equal to 1?

d. What is the distinguishing characteristic of a slide-wire type Wheatstone bridge?

e. Why are a-c generators and headphones used in reactive bridge circuits instead of batteries and galvanometers?

f. What changes must be made in a capacitive bridge circuit when measuring an electrolytic capacitor?

g. Explain the difference between dissipation factor and storage factor.

h. If capacitive bridges use capacitors as the standard, then why do not inductive bridges use inductors as the standard?

i. What are the mathematical relationships for determining an unknown resistor, capacitor, and inductor in a bridge circuit?

j. What is a storage factor?

ELECTRICAL CIRCUIT DIAGRAMS

Section I. COMMON MARKINGS AND SYMBOLS USED ON ELECTRICAL CIRCUIT DIAGRAMS

C-1. Common Markings to Designate Functions

Common markings are used on electrical circuit diagrams to designate the functional use of a device. Table C-1 gives a list of markings most frequently used.

Table C-1. Common Markings Used to Designate Functions

Device	Contractor designation	Relay designation	Other equipment designation
Accelerating	A	AR	
Ammeter switch			AS
Autotransformer			AT
Brake	B	BR	
Capacitor			C
Circuit breaker			CB
Closing coil		CCR	CC
Control		CR	
Control switch			CS
Counter EMF		CEMF	
Current limit		CLR	
Current transformer			CT
Down	D		
Dynamic braking	DB	DBR	
Emergency switch			ES
Exciter field	EF	EFR	
Field	F	FR	
Field accelerating	FA	FAR	
Field discharge	FD	FDR	
Field economy	FE	FER	
Field loss (failure)	FL	FLR	
Field weakening	FW	FWR	
Float flow switch			FS
Forward	F	FR	
Full field	FF	FFR	
Ground detector			GD
High speed	HS	HSR	
Hoist	H	HR	
Jam, jog	J	JR	
Kickoff	KO	KOR	
Limit switch			LS
Lowering	L	LR	
Low speed	LS	LSR	
Main breaker			MB
Master switch			MS
Motor circuit switch			MCS

Table C-1. Common Markings Used to Designate Functions—Continued

Device	Contractor designation	Relay designation	Other equipment designation
Motor field			MF
Overload		OL	
Oversupeed		OSR	
Overspeed switch			OSS
Plugging	P	PR	
Plugging forward		PF	
Plugging reverse		PR	
Potential transformer			PT
Power factor		PFR	
Power factor meter			PF
Pushbutton			PB
Rectifier			REC
Resistor			RES
Reverse, run, raise	R		
Sequence protective		SPR	
Slow down		SR	
Squirrel-cage protective		SCR	
Start	S		
Switch			SW
Time closing			TC
Time opening			TO
Time relay		TR	
Transfer relay		TRR	
Trip coil			TC
Undervoltage	UV	UVR	
Up	U		
Voltage regulator		VRG	
Voltmeter switch			VS

C-2. Power-Terminal Markings

Common markings for designating power terminals on electrical circuit diagrams consist of a capital letter followed by a suffix numeral. If a multiplicity of equal devices are used, they are further designated by a numeral followed by a letter. Thus, 1A and 2A are device designations. A_1 and A_2 are terminal markings. Table C-2 gives a partial list of terminal markings.

Table C-2. Power-Terminal Markings

	Direct current	Alternating current
Brake	B1, B2, B3	B1, B2, B3.
Brush on commutator (armature).	A1, A2	A1, A2, A3.
Brush on slipring (rotor)		M1, M2, M3.
Field (series)	S1, S2	
Field (shunt)	F1, F2	F1, F2.
Line	L1, L2	L1, L2, L3.
Resistance (armature)	R1, R2, R3	R1, R2, R3.
Resistance (shunt field)	V1, V2, V3	
Stator		T1, T2, T3.
Transformer (high voltage).		H1, H2, H3.
Transformer (low voltage).		X1, X2, X3.

C-3. Symbols

It is common practice to use symbols to designate various pieces of equipment and everyone recognizes the equipment represented by the symbols, although there may be no resemblance between the symbol and the physical appearance of the article represented. Figure C-1 shows a list of symbols generally used in electrical circuit diagrams.

NAME	SYMBOL
BATTERY	—⊣∣⊢ or —⊣∣⊢—
CAPACITOR, FIXED	—⊣⊢—
CIRCUIT BREAKERS	
AIR CIRCUIT BREAKER	
THREE-POLE POWER CIRCUIT BREAKER (SINGLE THROW)(WITH TERMINALS)	
THERMAL TRIP AIR CIRCUIT BREAKER	
COILS	
NON-MAGNETIC CORE-FIXED	
MAGNETIC CORE-FIXED	
MAGNETIC CORE-ADJUSTABLE TAP OR SLIDE WIRE	
OPERATING COIL	
BLOWOUT COIL	
BLOWOUT COIL WITH TERMINALS	
SERIES FIELD	
SHUNT FIELD	
COMMUTATING FIELD	

Figure C–1. Symbols of American Standards Association (1 of 5).

NAME	SYMBOL
CONNECTIONS (MECHANICAL)	
MECHANICAL CONNECTION OF SHIELD	-----
MECHANICAL INTERLOCK	—+—
DIRECT CONNECTED UNITS	O--O
CONNECTIONS (WIRING)	
ELECTRIC CONDUCTOR—CONTROL	———
ELECTRIC CONDUCTOR—POWER	▬▬▬
JUNCTION OF CONDUCTORS	o—
WIRING TERMINAL	o
GROUND	⏚
CROSSING OF CONDUCTORS — NOT CONNECTED	┼
CROSSING OF CONNECTED CONDUCTORS	┼
JOINING OF CONDUCTORS — NOT CROSSING	⊢ ⊣
CONTACTS (ELECTRICAL)	
NORMALLY CLOSED CONTACT (NC)	
NORMALLY OPEN CONTACT (NO)	

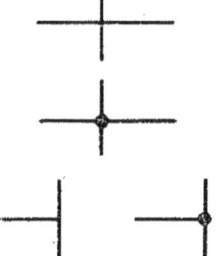

NO CONTACT WITH TIME CLOSING (TC) FEATURE	
NC CONTACT WITH TIME OPENING (TO) FEATURE	

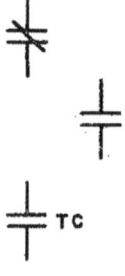

NOTE: NO (NORMALLY OPEN) AND NC (NORMALLY CLOSED) DESIGNATES THE POSITION OF THE CONTACTS WHEN THE MAIN DEVICE IS IN THE DE-ENERGIZED OR NONOPERATED POSITION.

Figure C-1—Continued—(2 of 5).

NAME	SYMBOL

CONTACTOR, SINGLE-POLE, ELECTRICALLY OPERATED, WITH BLOWOUT COIL

  NOTE: FUNDAMENTAL SYMBOLS FOR CONTACTS, COILS, MECHANICAL CONNECTIONS, etc., ARE THE BASIS OF CONTACTOR SYMBOLS

FUSE

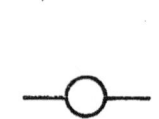

INDICATING LIGHTS

    INDICATING LAMP WITH LEADS

    INDICATING LAMP WITH TERMINALS

INSTRUMENTS

    AMMETER, WITH TERMINALS

    VOLTMETER, WITH TERMINALS

    WATTMETER, WITH TERMINALS

MACHINES (ROTATING)

    MACHINE OR ROTATING ARMATURE

    SQUIRREL-CAGE INDUCTION MOTOR

    WOUND-ROTOR INDUCTION MOTOR OR GENERATOR

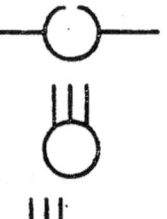

    SYNCHRONOUS MOTOR, GENERATOR OR CONDENSER

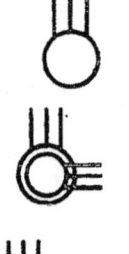

    D-C COMPOUND MOTOR OR GENERATOR

    NOTE: COMMUTATING, SERIES, AND SHUNT FIELDS MAY BE INDICATED BY 1, 2 AND 3 ZIGZAGS RESPECTIVELY. SERIES AND SHUNT COILS MAY BE INDICATED BY HEAVY AND LIGHT LINES OR 1 AND 2 ZIGZAGS RESPECTIVELY.

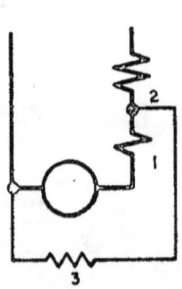

Figure C–1—Continued—(3 of 5).

NAME	SYMBOL
WINDING SYMBOLS	
THREE PHASE WYE (UNGROUNDED)	
THREE PHASE WYE (GROUNDED)	
THREE PHASE DELTA	
NOTE: WINDING SYMBOLS MAY BE SHOWN IN CIRCLES FOR ALL MOTOR AND GENERATOR SYMBOLS.	
RECTIFIER, DRY OR ELECTROLYTIC, FULL WAVE	FULL WAVE
RELAYS	
OVERCURRENT OR OVERVOLTAGE RELAY WITH 1 NO CONTACT	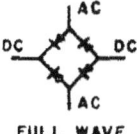 OR
THERMAL OVERLOAD RELAY HAVING 2 SERIES HEATING ELEMENTS AND 1 NC CONTACT	OR 
RESISTORS	
RESISTOR, FIXED, WITH LEADS	
RESISTOR, FIXED, WITH TERMINALS	
RESISTOR, ADJUSTABLE TAP OR SLIDE WIRE	
RESISTOR, ADJUSTABLE BY FIXED LEADS	
RESISTOR, ADJUSTABLE BY FIXED TERMINALS	
INSTRUMENT OR RELAY SHUNT	
SWITCHES	
KNIFE SWITCH, SINGLE-POLE (SP)	
KNIFE SWITCH, DOUBLE-POLE SINGLE-THROW (DPST)	

Figure C–1—Continued—(4 of 5).

NAME	SYMBOL
SWITCHES (CONTINUED)	
KNIFE SWITCH, TRIPLE-POLE SINGLE-THROW (TPST)	
KNIFE SWITCH, SINGLE-POLE DOUBLE-THROW (SPDT)	
KNIFE SWITCH, DOUBLE-POLE DOUBLE-THROW (DPDT)	
KNIFE SWITCH, TRIPLE-POLE DOUBLE-THROW (TPDT)	
FIELD-DISCHARGE SWITCH WITH RESISTOR	
PUSHBUTTON, NORMALLY OPEN (NO)	
PUSHBUTTON NORMALLY CLOSED (NC)	
PUSHBUTTON OPEN AND CLOSED (SPRING-RETURN)	
NORMALLY CLOSED LIMIT SWITCH CONTACT	LS
NORMALLY OPEN LIMIT SWITCH CONTACT	LS
THERMAL ELEMENT	
TRANSFORMERS	
1 PHASE TWO-WINDING TRANSFORMER	
AUTOTRANSFORMER SINGLE-PHASE	

Figure C-1—Continued—(5 of 5).

Section II. REPAIR SHOP DIAGRAMS

C-4. Introduction

Electrical circuit diagrams are essential to a repairman's work. Many electrical circuit diagrams use in a repair shop are connection diagrams and controller diagrams. These diagrams are a form of pictorial shorthand which uses symbols rather than pictures of electrical equipment to indicate how separate pieces of electrical equipment are connected in a circuit to perform useful electromechanical functions.

C-5. Types of Repair Shop Diagrams

a. Schematic Diagrams. A simple form of repair shop diagram is a schematic diagram like the ones shown in figures C-2, C-3, and C4. Such a diagram shows how the lead wires from the windings of a generator or motor are connected to the power line.

b. Block Diagram. Both the circular and flat (extended) types of diagrams indicate the number of poles and the connection of the lead wires

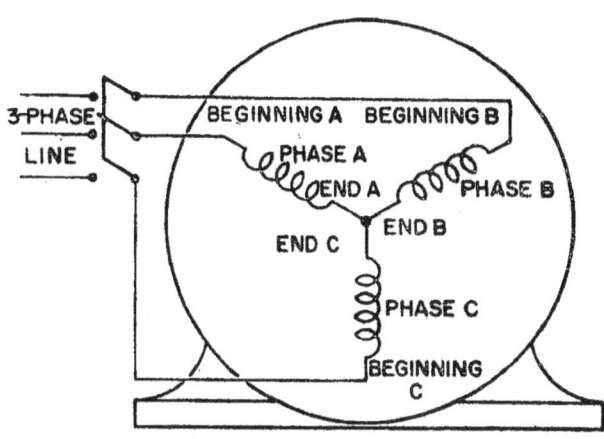

Figure C-4. Schematic wiring diagram of a star-connected, polyphase motor.

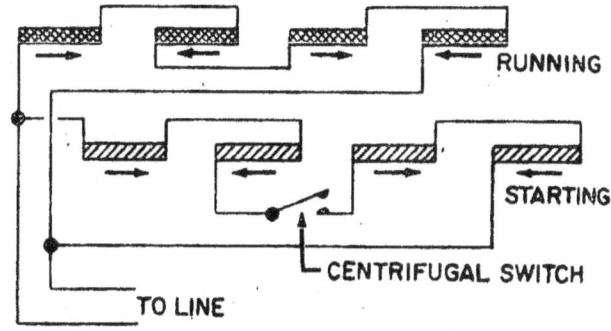

Figure C-5. Block diagram (extended type) of a four-pole, split-phase motor.

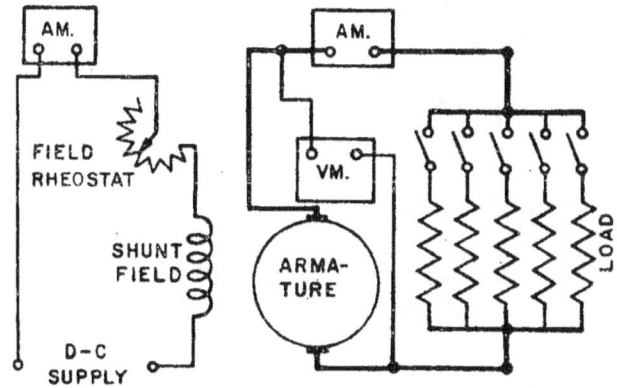

Figure C-2. Schematic wiring diagram of a separately excited generator.

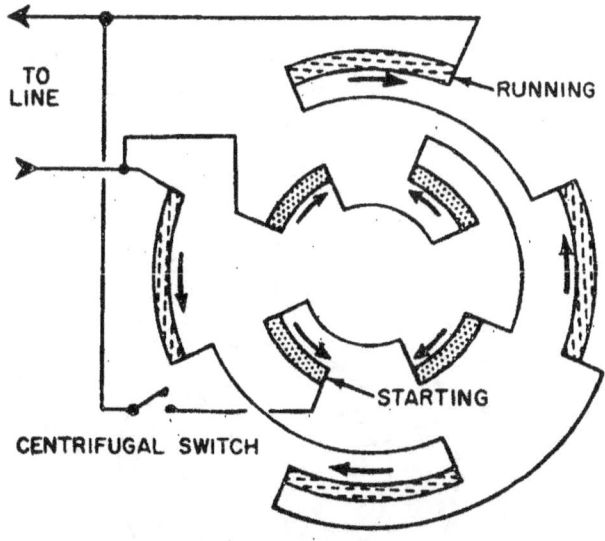

Figure C-6. Circular block diagram of a four-pole, split-phase motor.

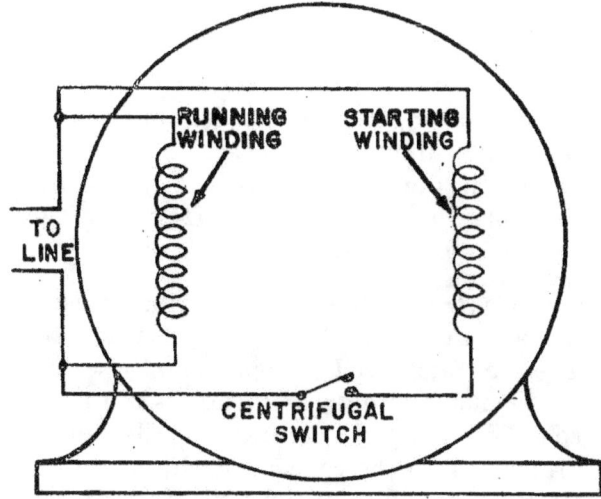

Figure C-3. Schematic wiring diagram of a split-phase motor.

from the windings to the power line (fig C-5, C-6, C-7, and C-8).

c. Connection Diagrams. The connection diagrams appearing in this manual should be used as a guide in developing an actual diagram of the unit under repair. At the time preliminary

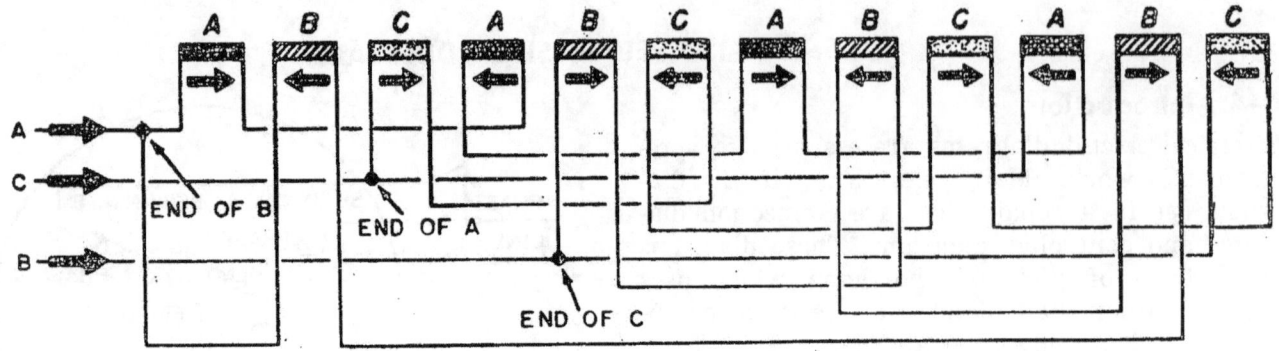

Figure C-7. Block diagram (extended type) of three-phase, four-pole, series-delta motor.

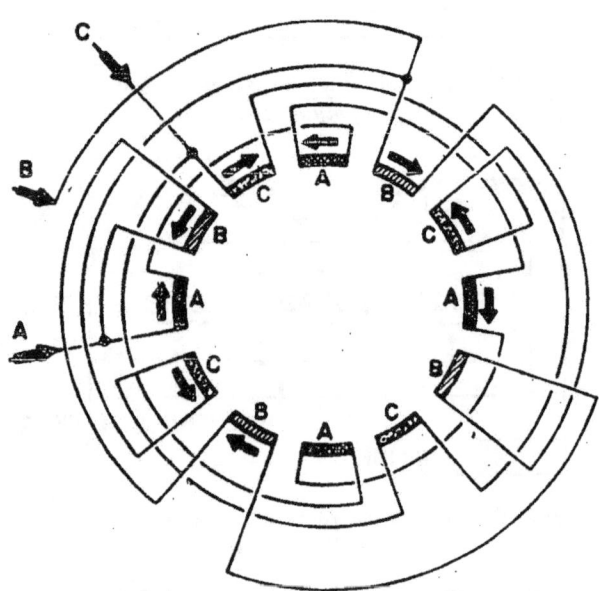

Figure C-8. Circular block diagram of a four-pole, three-phase, series-delta motor.

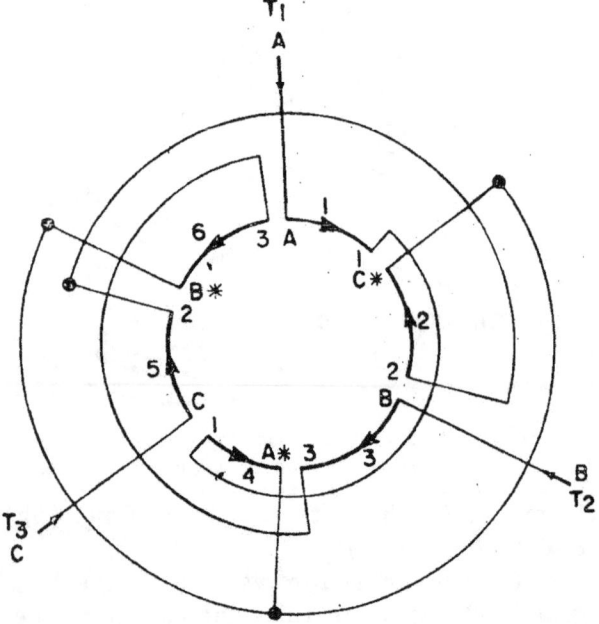

Figure C-9. Two-pole, three-phase, series-star connection.

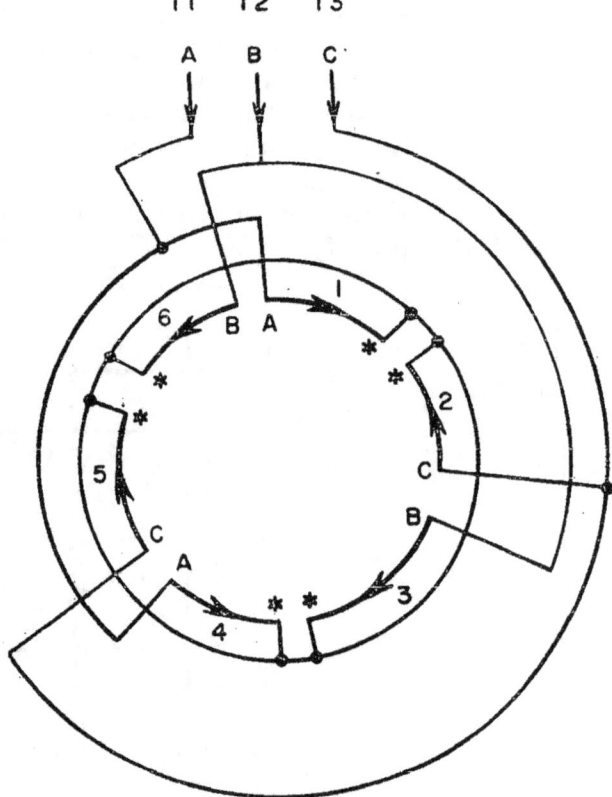

Figure C-10. Two-pole, three-phase, two-parallel-star connection.

data is taken, a diagram is developed for the particular unit under repair. For repair work, the block diagram is used to best advantage. Examples of connection diagrams are given in figures C-9 to C-21.

d. Controller Diagrams. Various types of controllers are used to run electrical machinery. The diagrams used to represent these controllers are elementary diagrams (fig C-22 to C-40) and complete wiring diagrams. Elementary diagrams reduce the concept of the operation to the simplest possible form by placing all parts necessary for the electromechanical operation of the

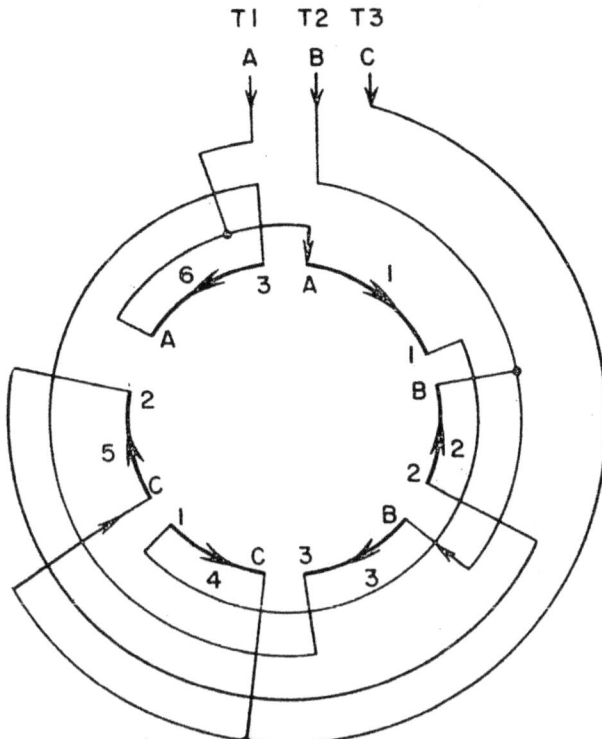

Figure C–11. Two-pole, three-phase, series-delta connection.

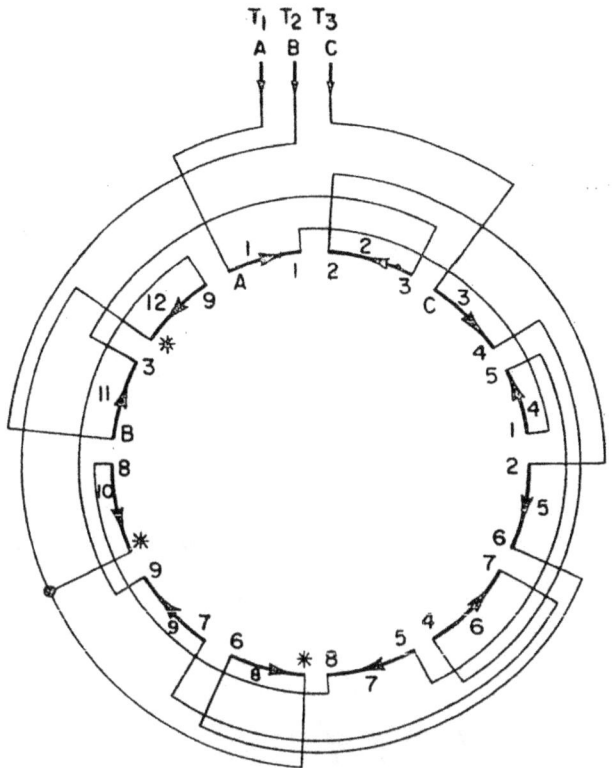

Figure C–13. Four-pole, three-phase, series-star connection.

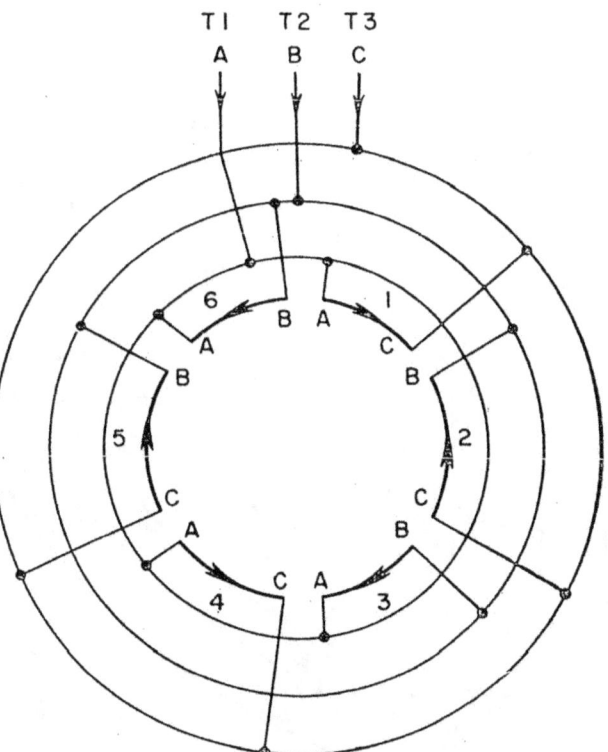

Figure C–12. Two-pole, three-phase, two-parallel-delta connection.

equipment in proximity to each other for clarity. In some elementary diagrams, however, where it is not possible to show all parts of the same equipment near to each other, code letters are used to designate the associated parts. For example, in figure C–24, coil M is used to operate main and auxiliary contractors M. Such a relationship between parts bearing the same designating letter must be remembered in studying elementary electrical circuit diagrams.

e. Wiring Diagram. Wiring diagrams indicate the actual relative position and connection of each wire, terminal, and component part of the electrical equipment. This type of diagram is illustrated in figures C–41, C–42, and C–43.

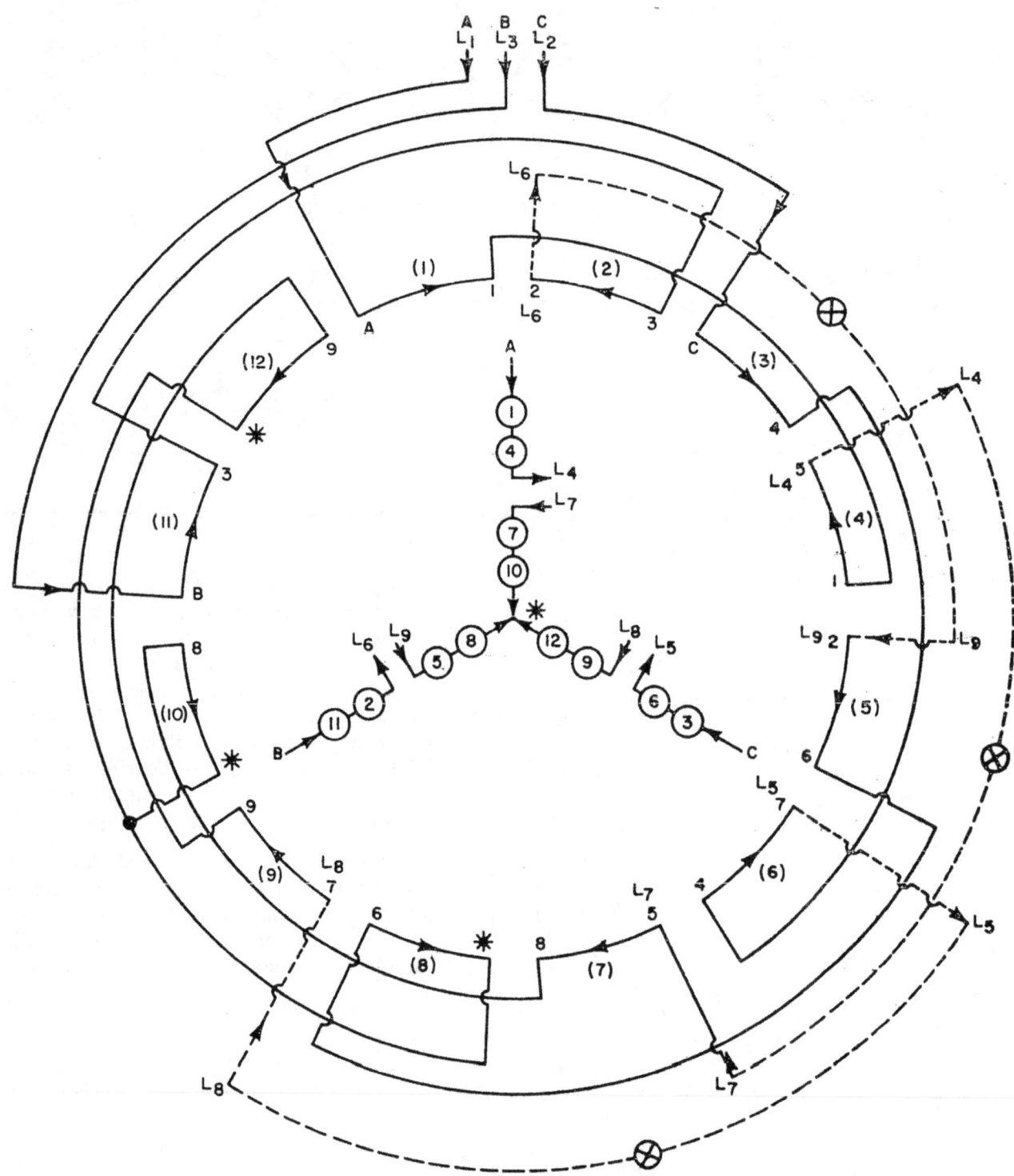

Figure C-14. Four-pole, three-phase, with three or nine leads for series-star or two-parallel-star connection.

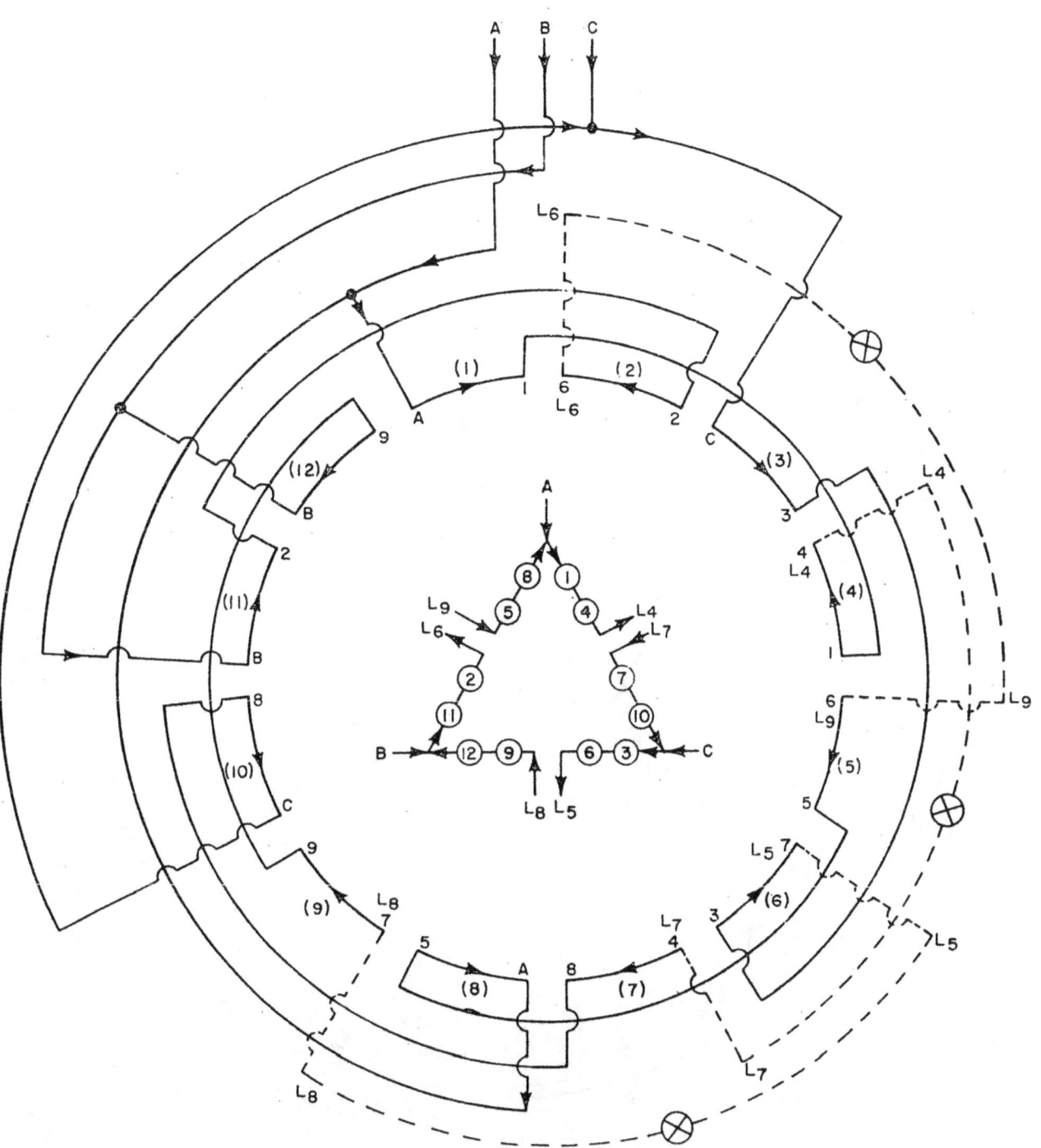

Figure C-15. Four-pole, three-phase, with three or nine leads for series-delta or two-parallel-delta connection.

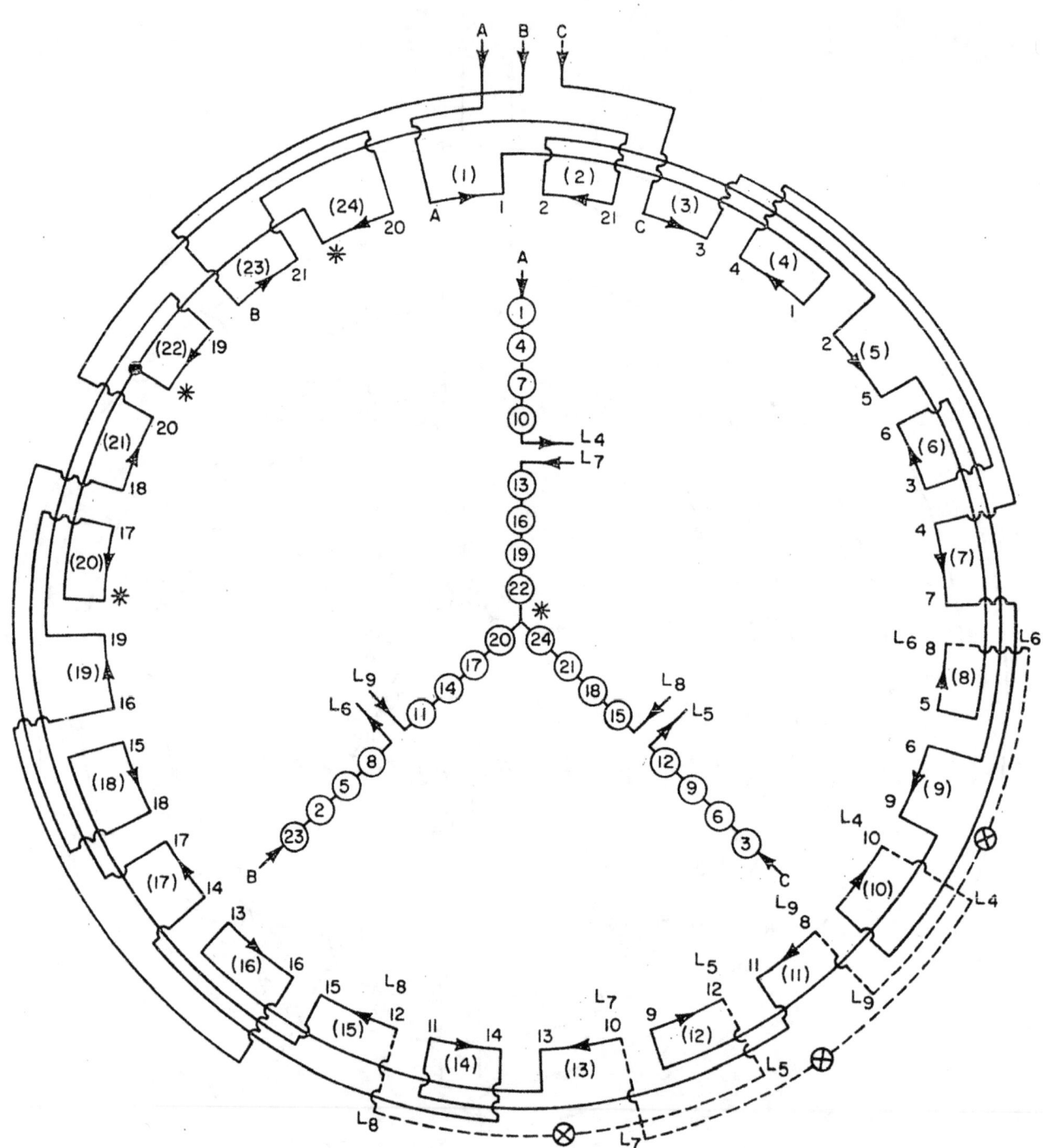

Figure C-16. Eight-pole, three-phase, with three or nine leads for series-star or parallel-star connection.

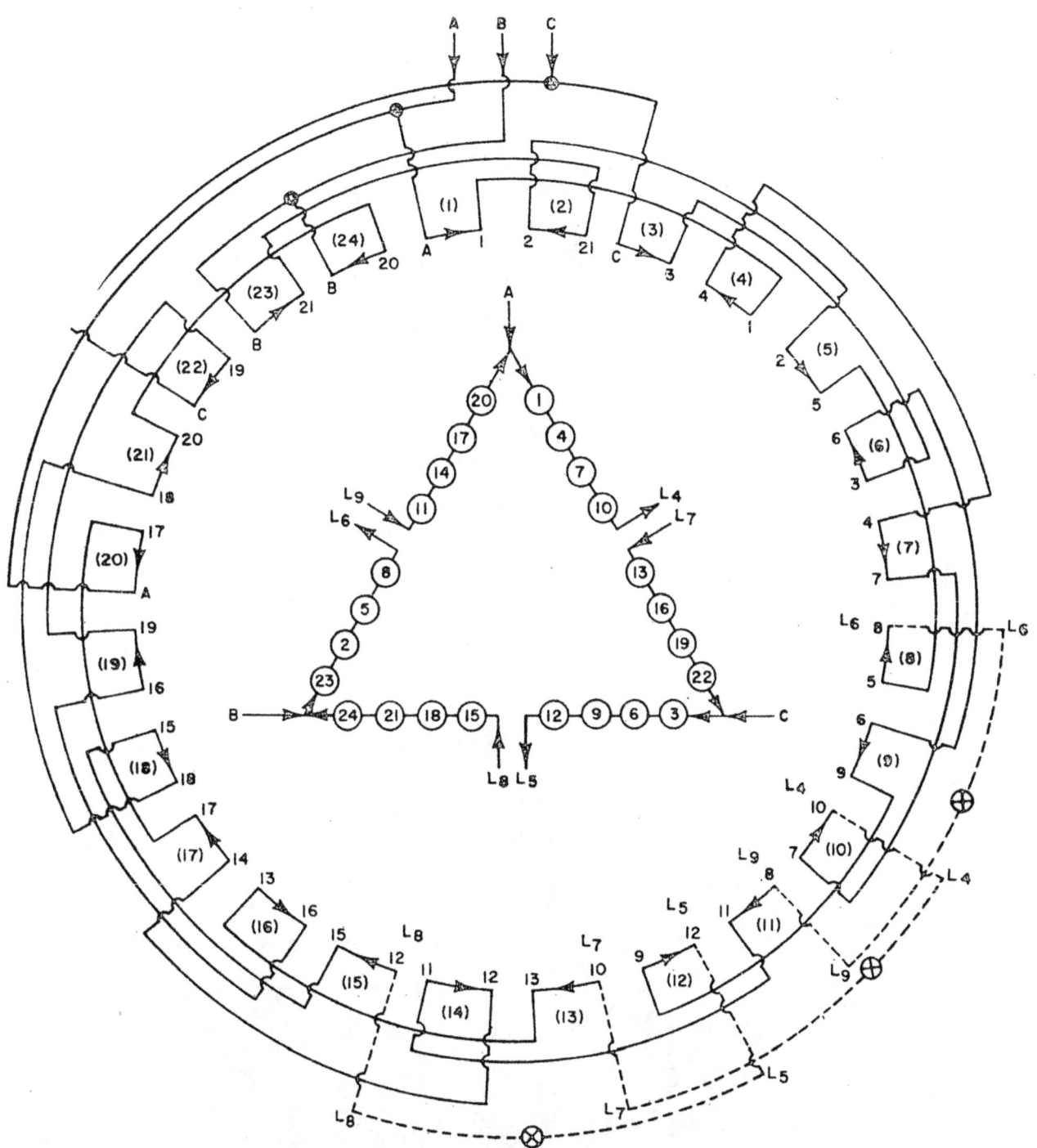

Figure C–17. Eight-pole, three-phase, with three or nine leads for series-delta or parallel-delta connection.

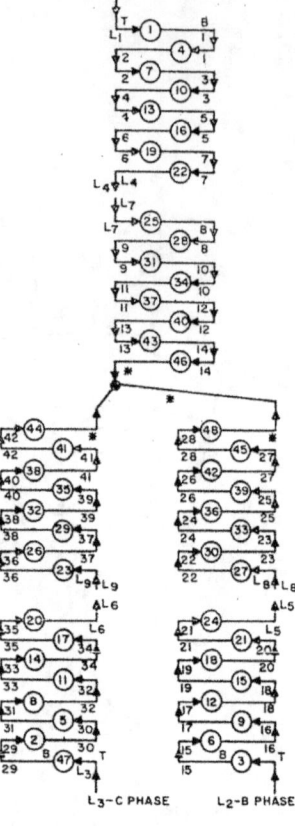

Figure C–18. Sixteen-pole, three-phase, nine-lead, series-star, or two-parallel-star connection.

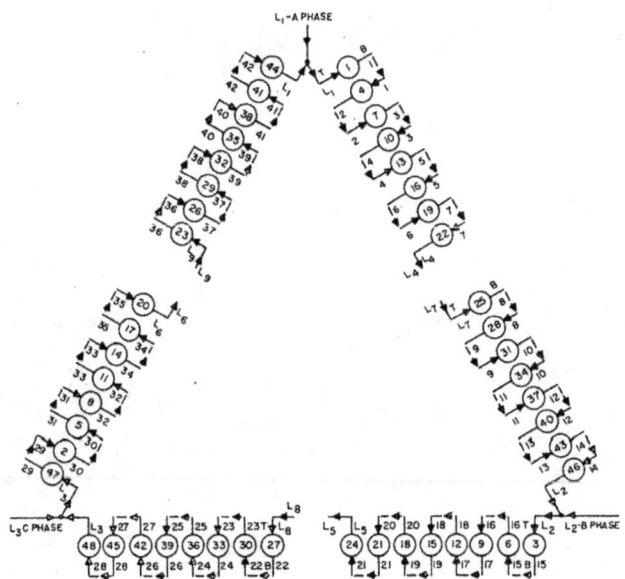

Figure C–19. Sixteen-pole, three-phase, nine-lead, series-delta, or two-parallel-delta connection.

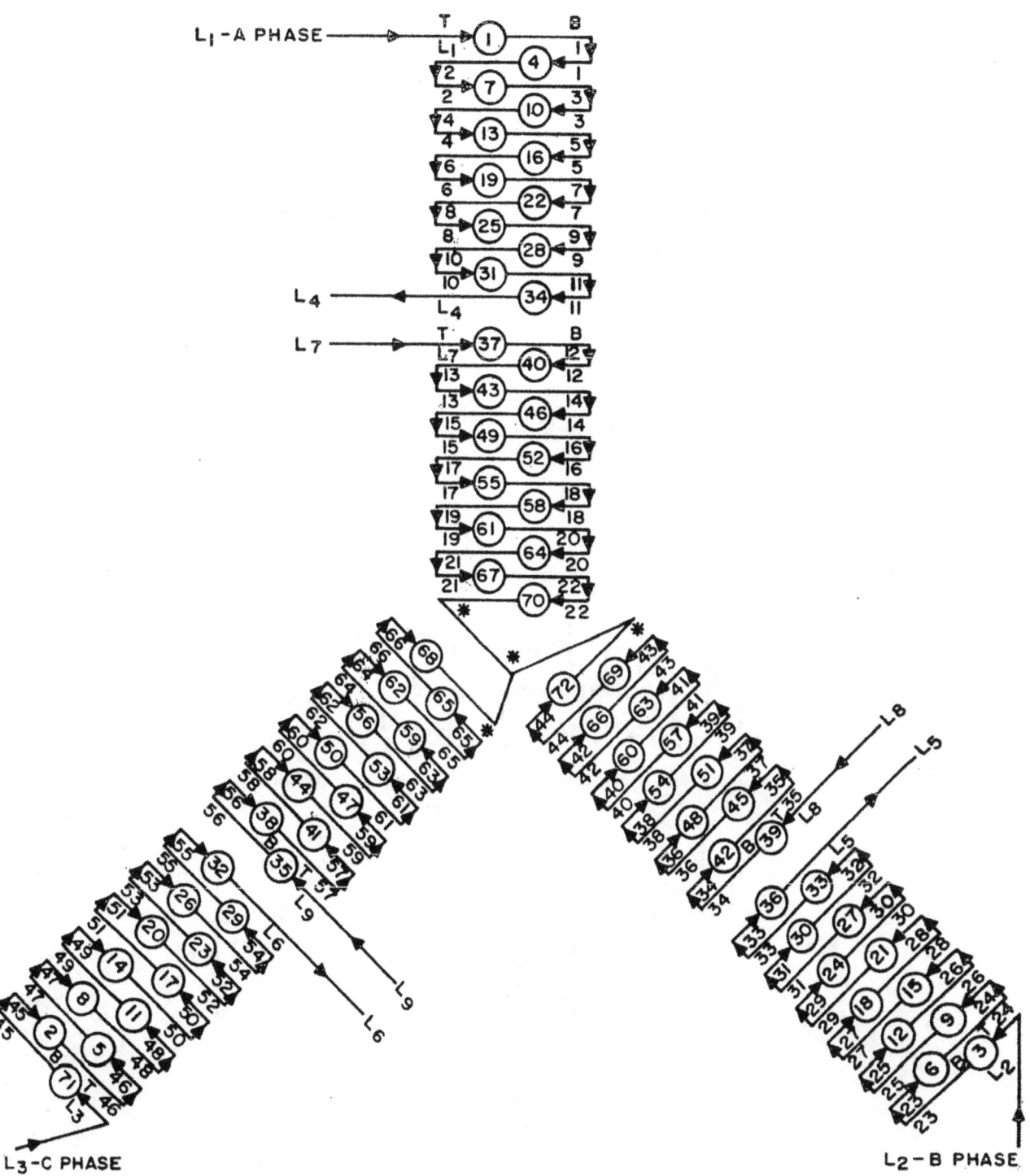

Figure C–20. Twenty-four-pole, three-phase, nine-lead, series-star, or two-parallel-star connection.

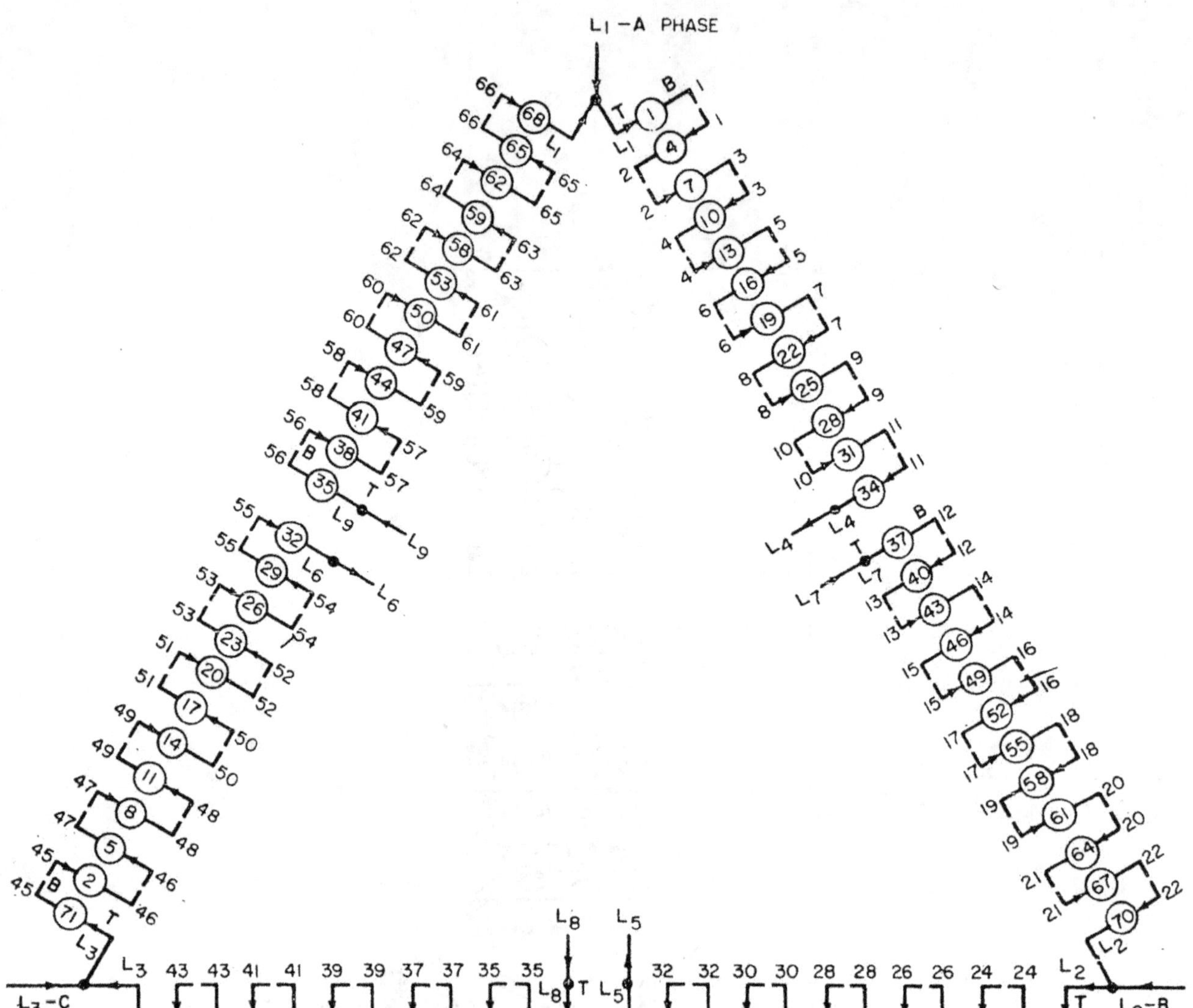

Figure C-21. *Twenty-four-pole, three-phase, nine-lead, series-delta, or two-parallel-delta connection.*

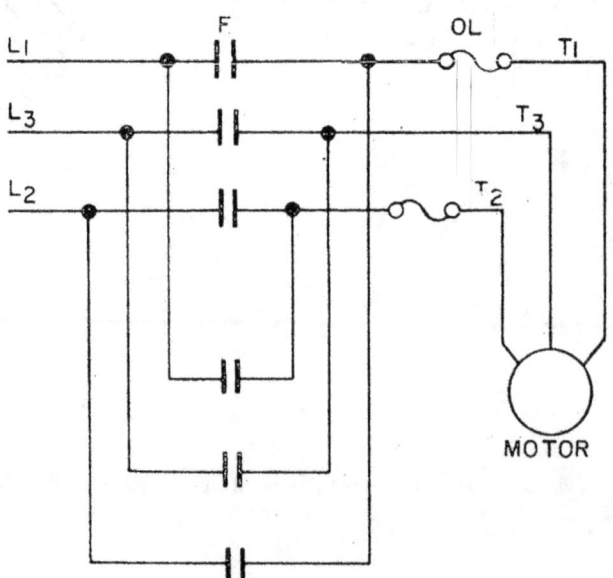

Figure C-22. *An elementary motor-driven-power circuit diagram for an ac motor.*

94

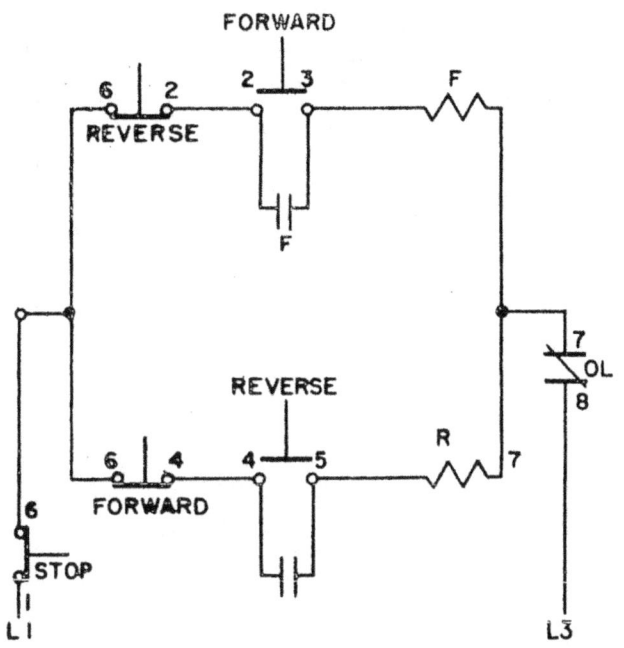

Figure C-23. An elementary motor-control circuit diagram for an ac motor.

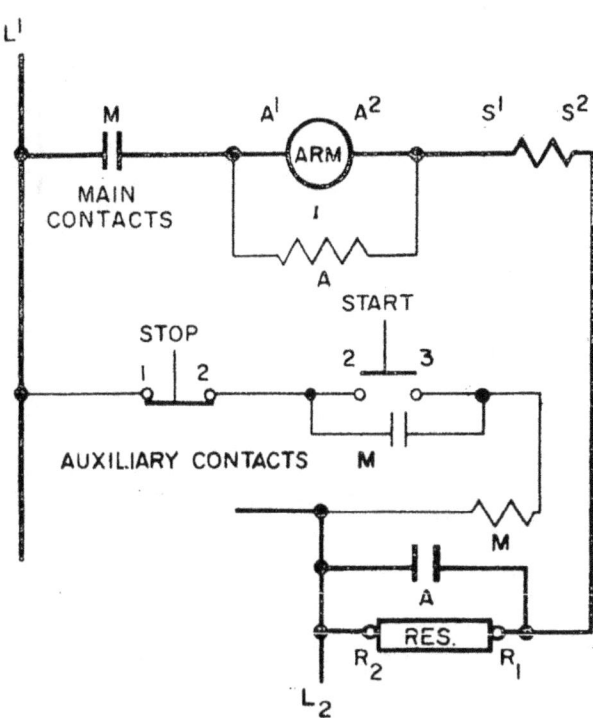

Figure C-24. An elementary control-and-power-circuit diagram for a dc motor.

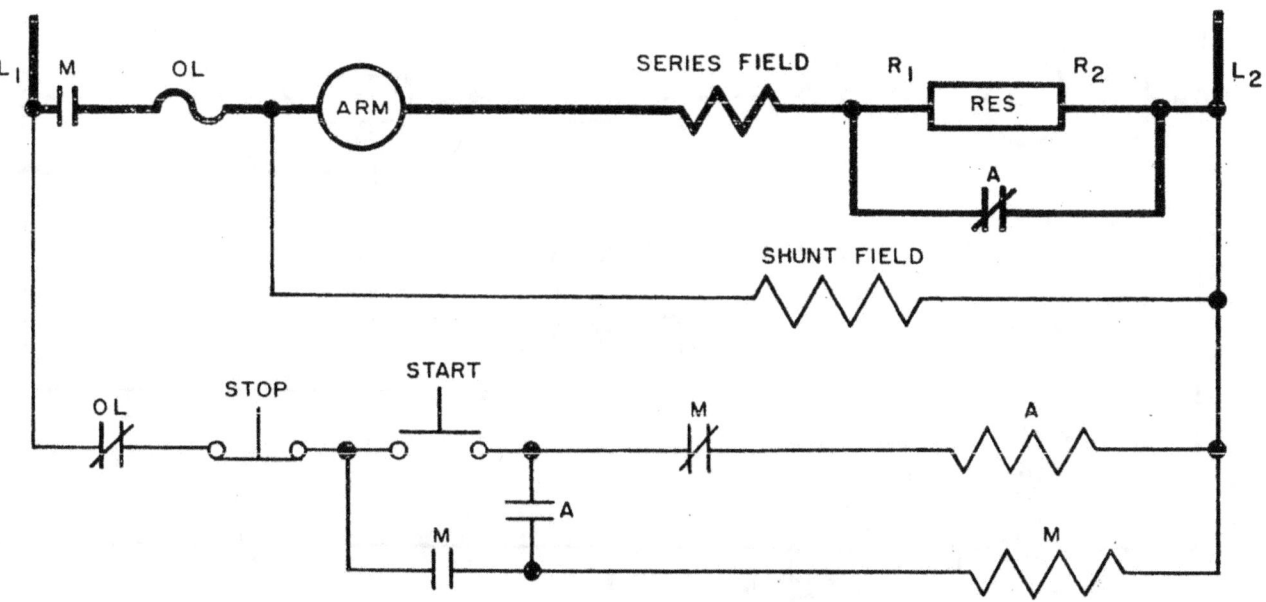

Figure C-25. An elementary schematic wiring diagram of a magnetic time-limit controller.

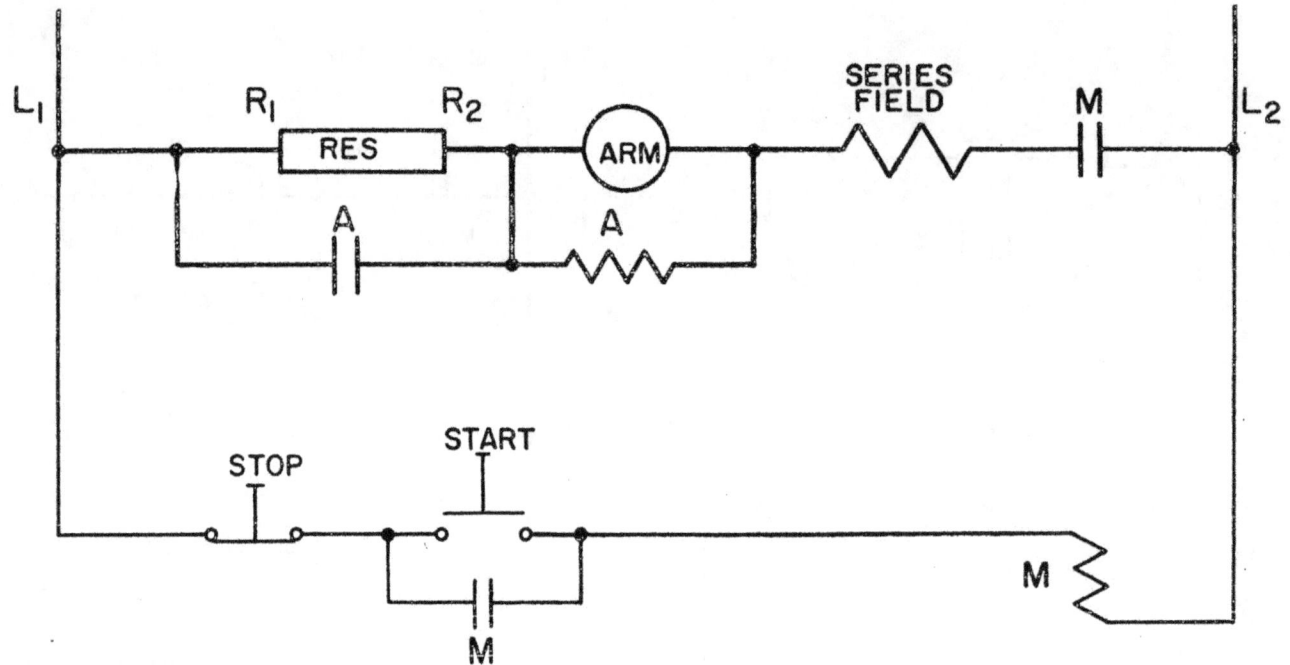

Figure C-26. An elementary schematic wiring diagram of a counter-emf controller.

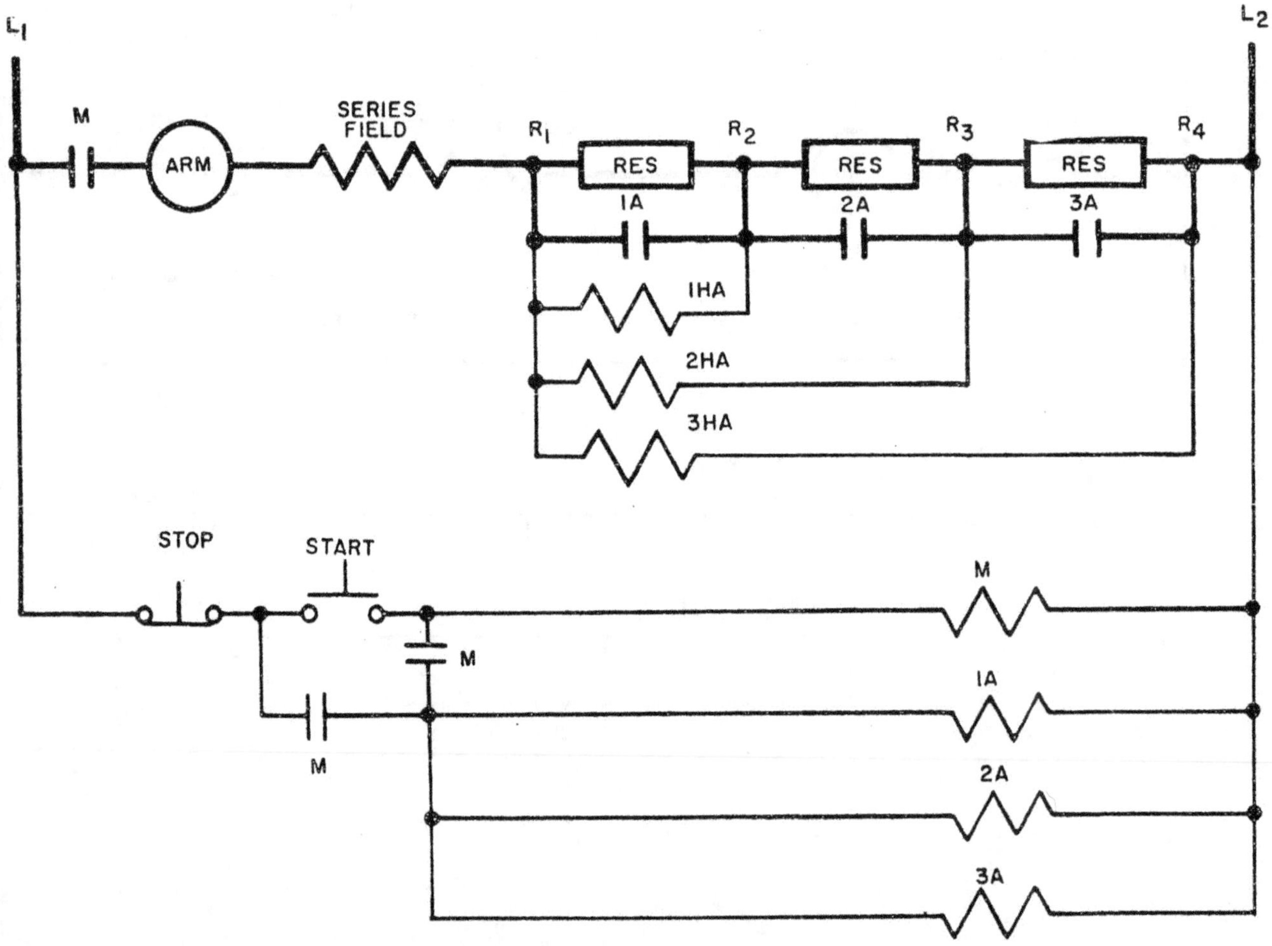

Figure C-27. An elementary schematic wiring diagram of a voltage-drop acceleration controller.

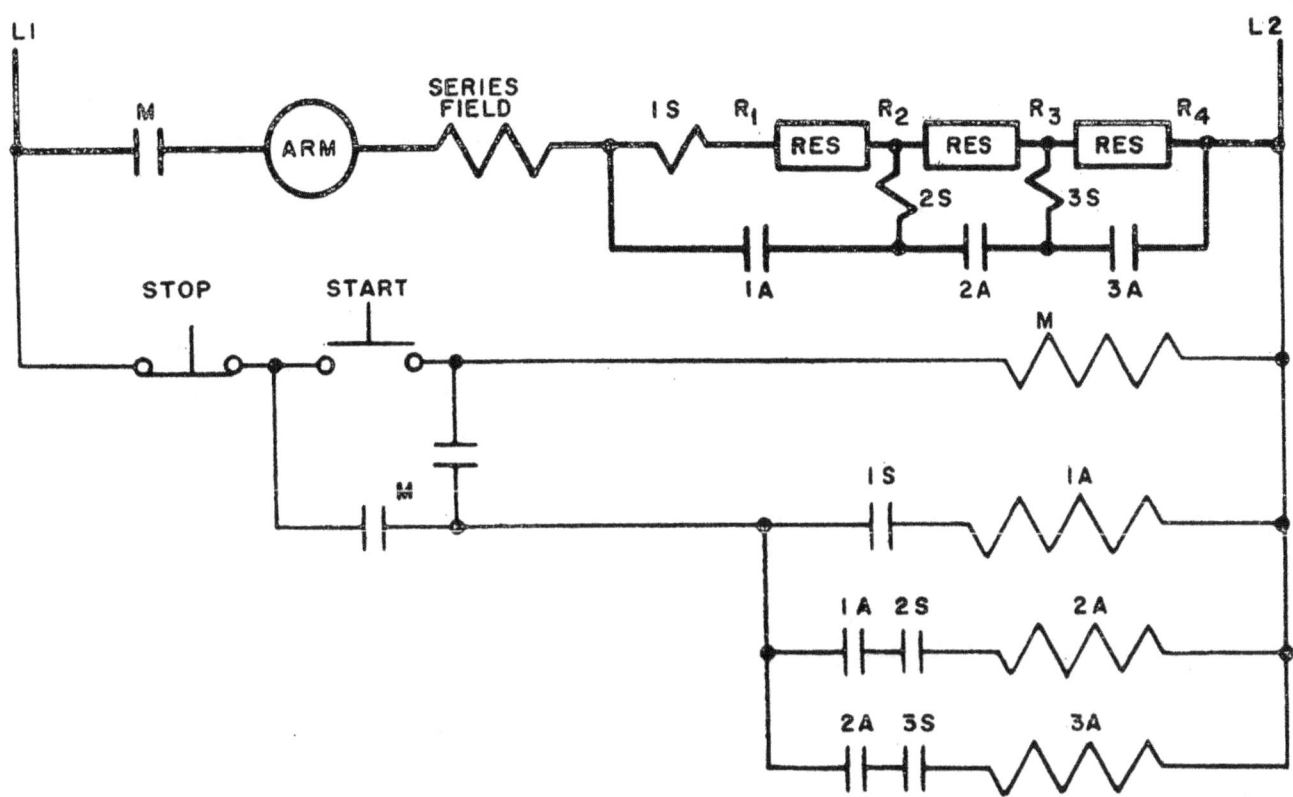

Figure C-28. An elementary schematic wiring diagram of a series-relay acceleration controller.

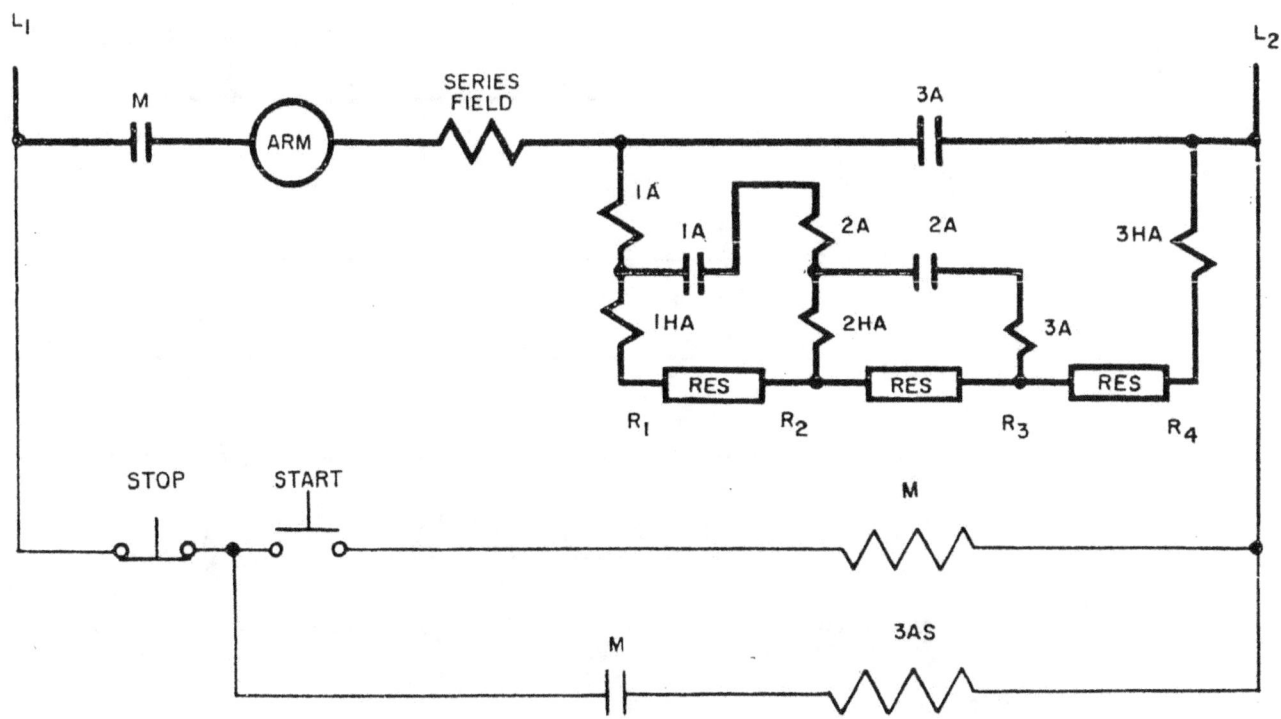

Figure C-29. An elementary schematic wiring diagram of a series-lockout-relay acceleration controller.

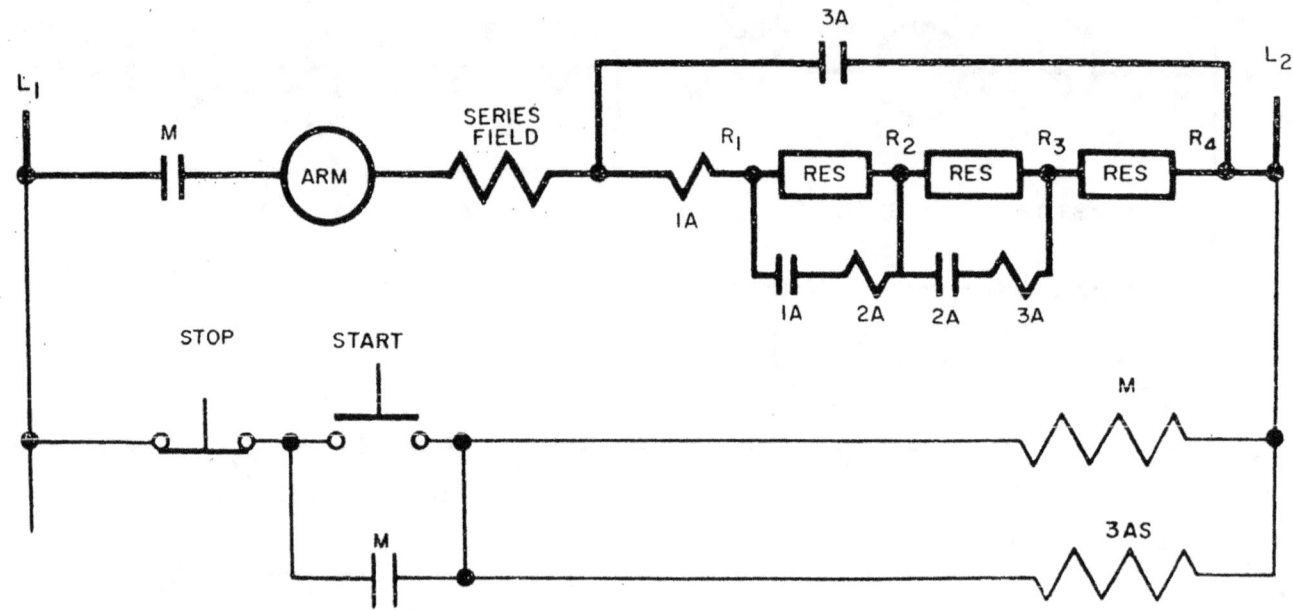

Figure C-30. An elementary schematic wiring diagram of a restricted iron-core lockout controller.

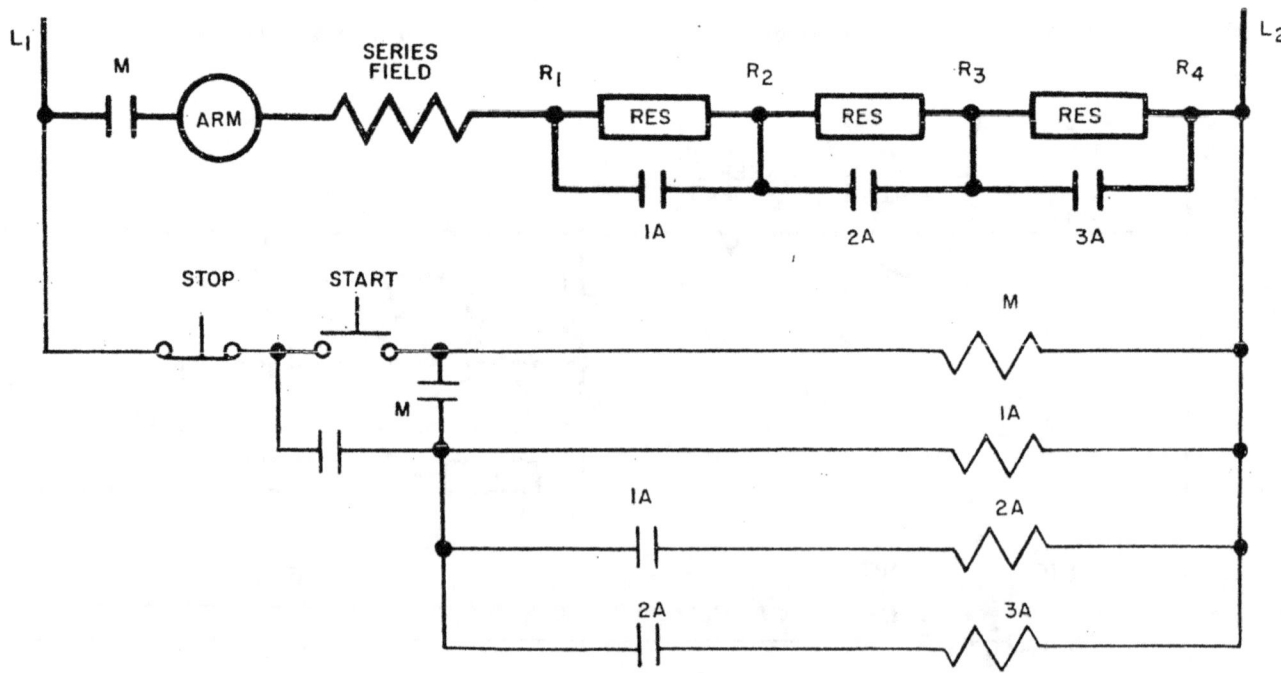

Figure C-31. An elementary schematic wiring diagram of an individual dashpot motor controller.

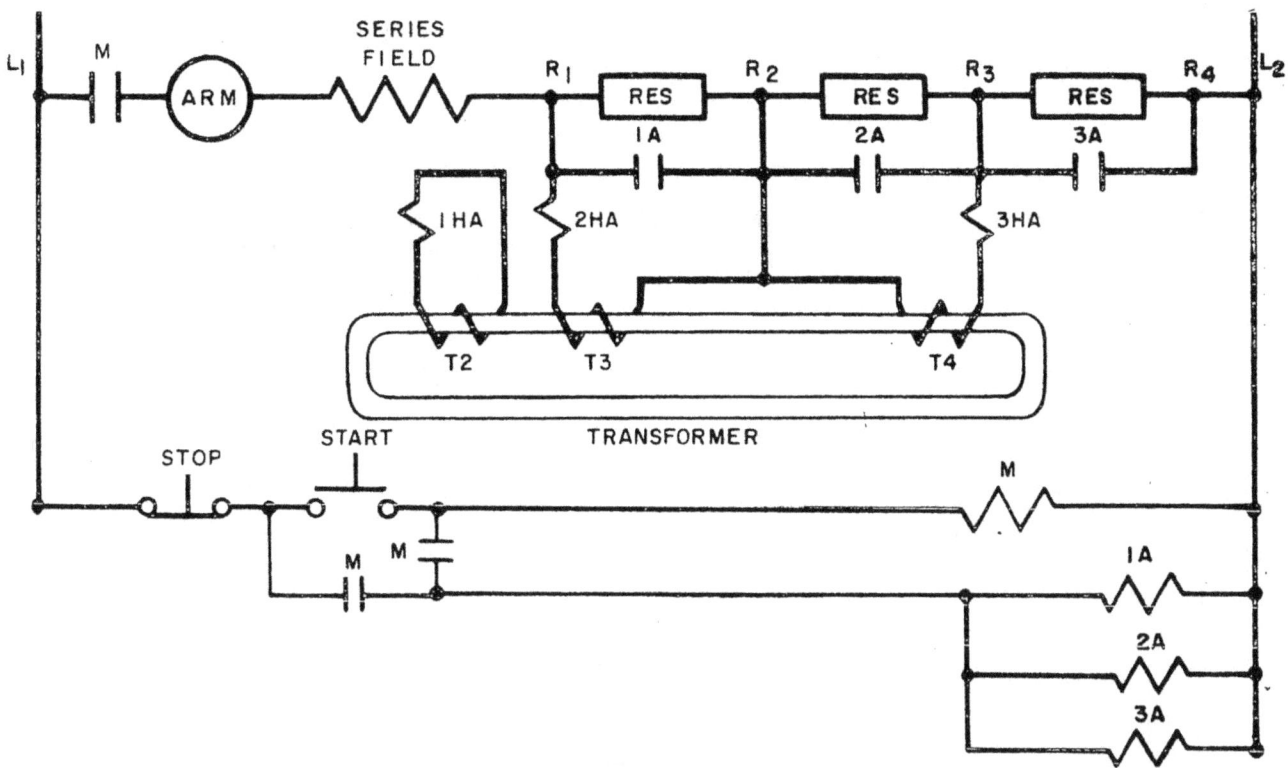

Figure C-32. An elementary schematic wiring diagram of an inductive time-limit controller.

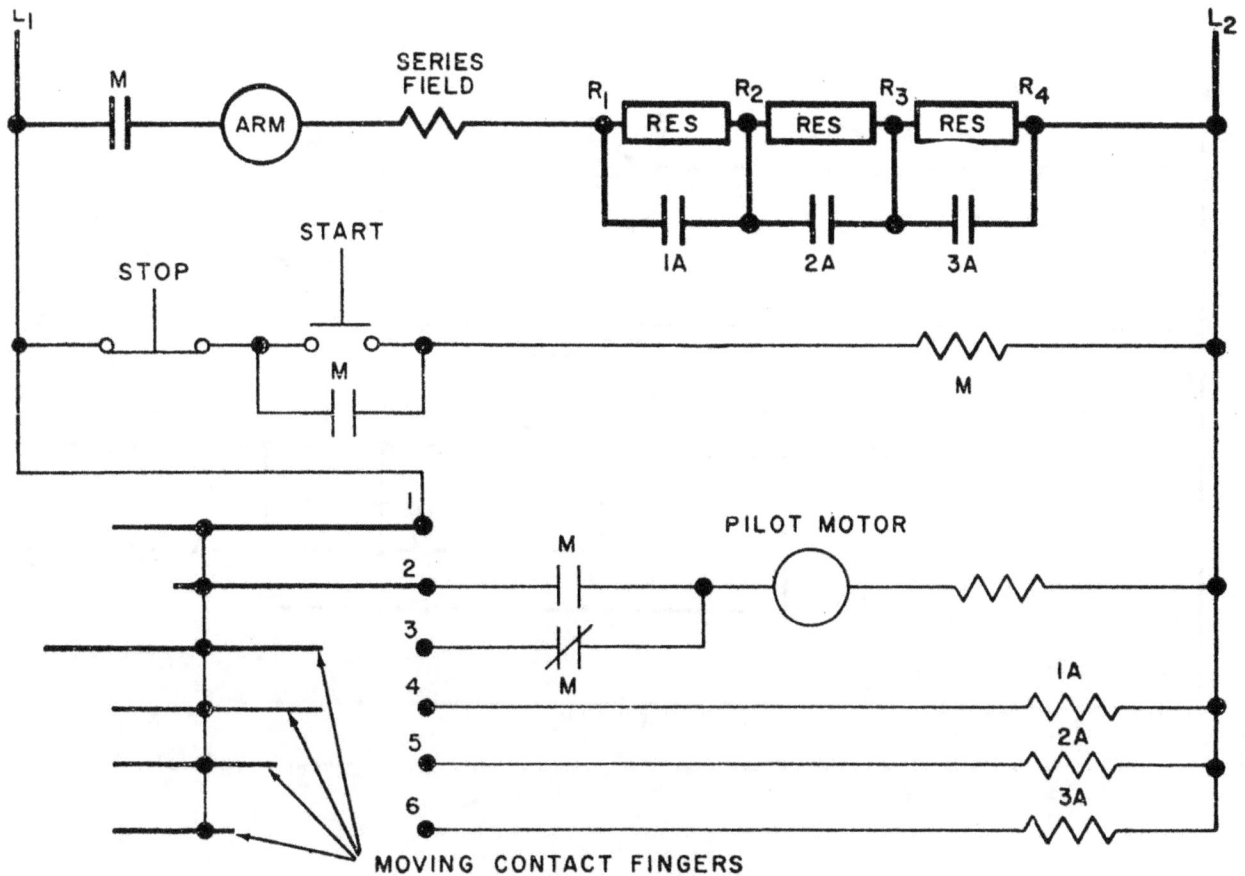

Figure C-33. An elementary schematic wiring diagram of a motor-driven time controller.

99

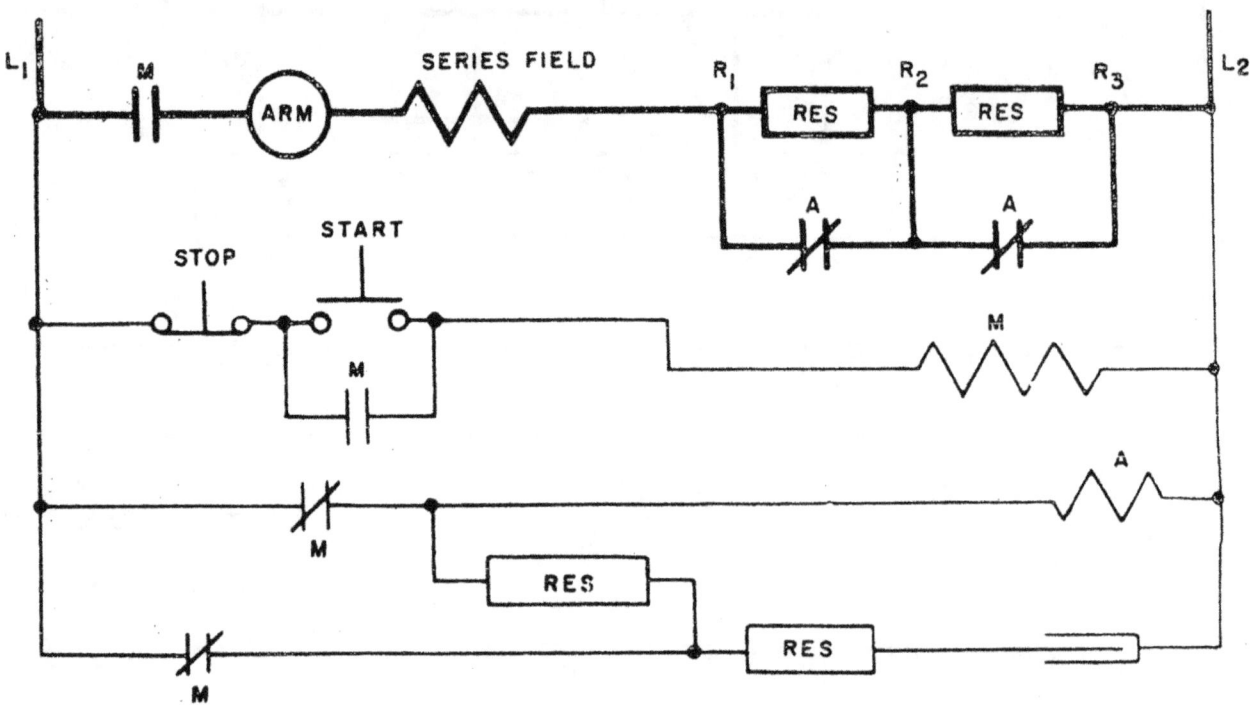

Figure C-34. An elementary schematic wiring diagram of a capacitor-timing starter.

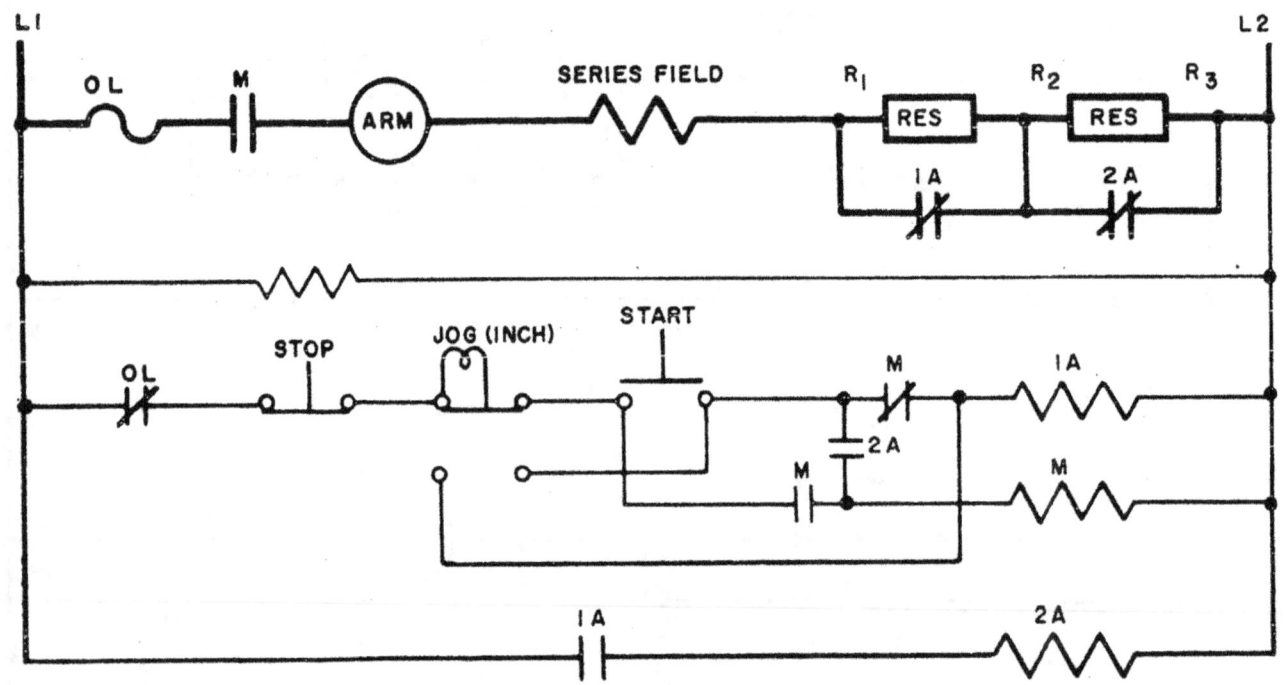

Figure C-35. An elementary schematic wiring diagram of a magnetic time-delay controller with jogging.

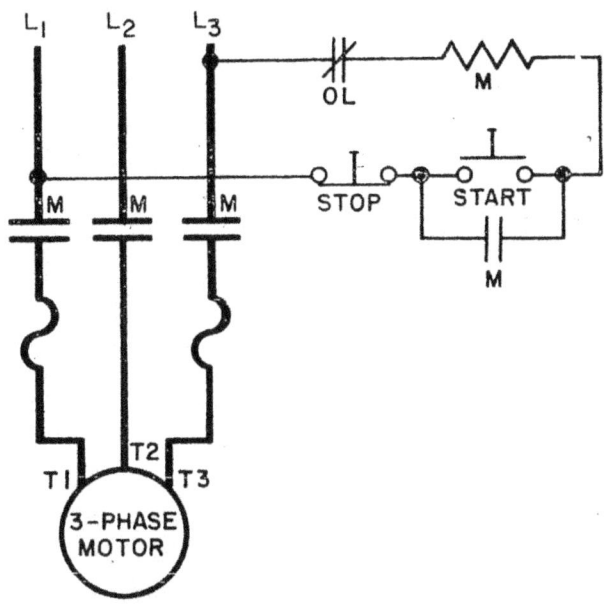

Figure C-36. An elementary schematic wiring diagram of a magnetic, ac, across-the-line starter.

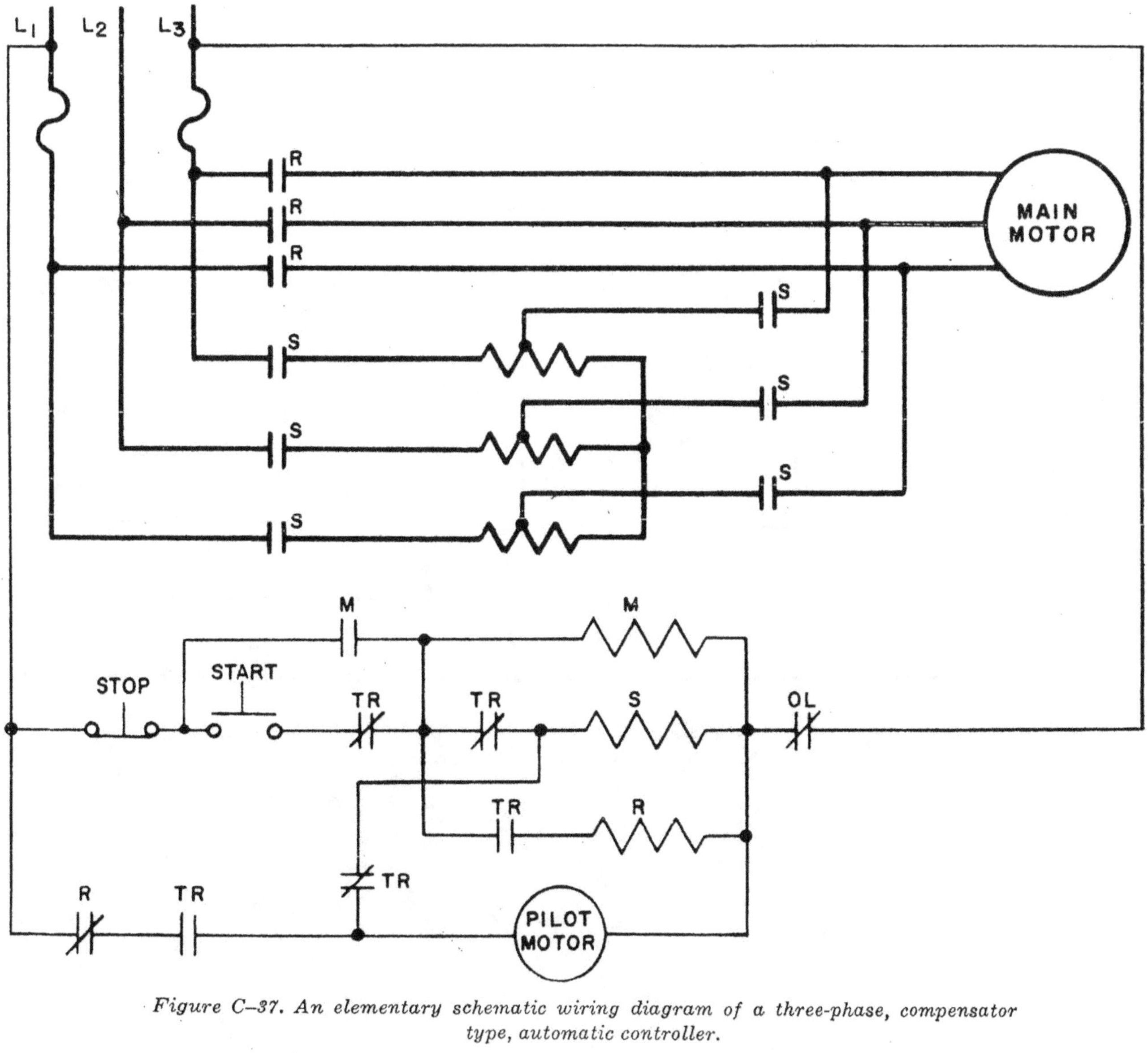

Figure C-37. An elementary schematic wiring diagram of a three-phase, compensator type, automatic controller.

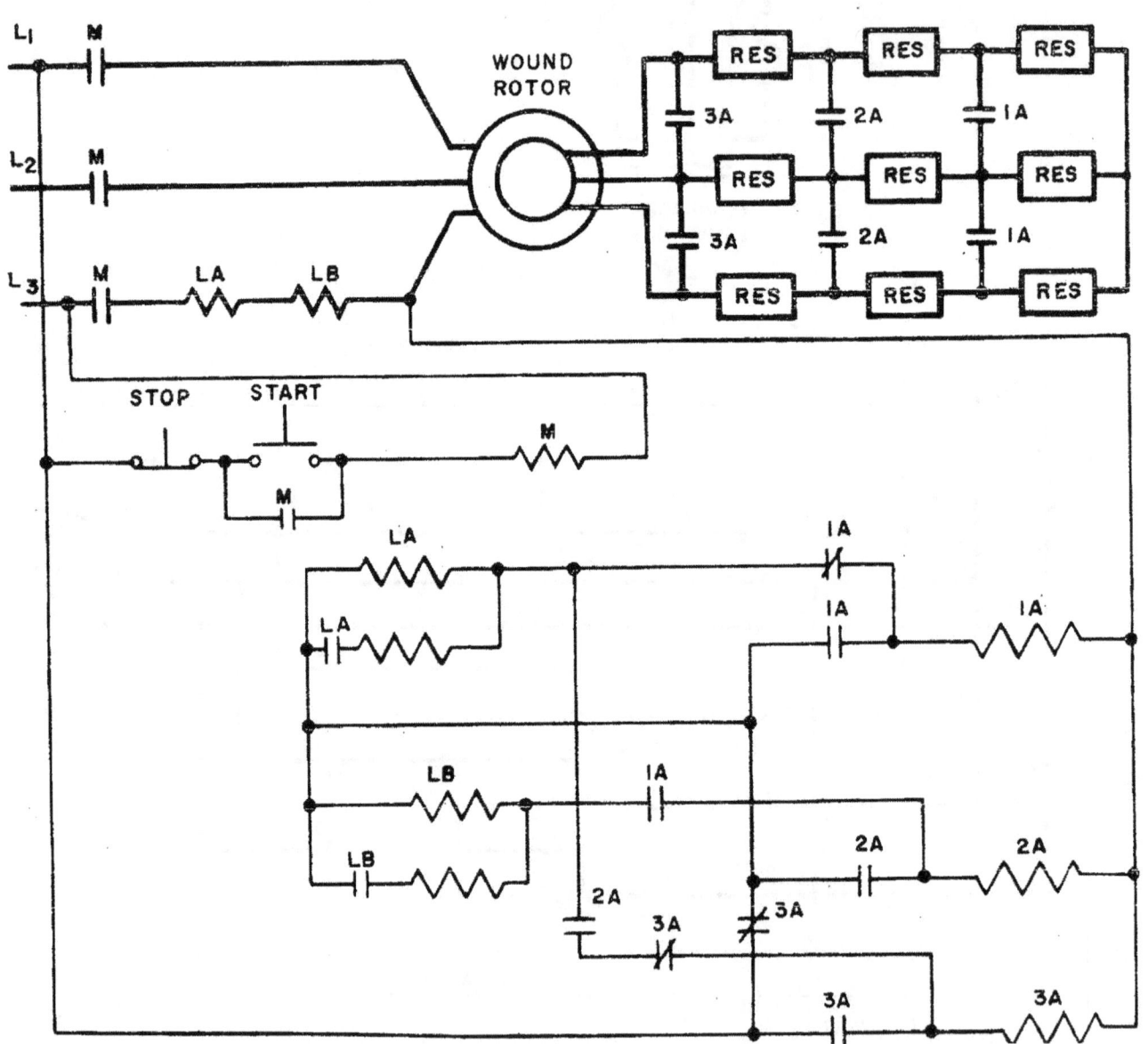

Figure C-38. An elementary schematic wiring diagram of a controller for a wound-rotor motor.

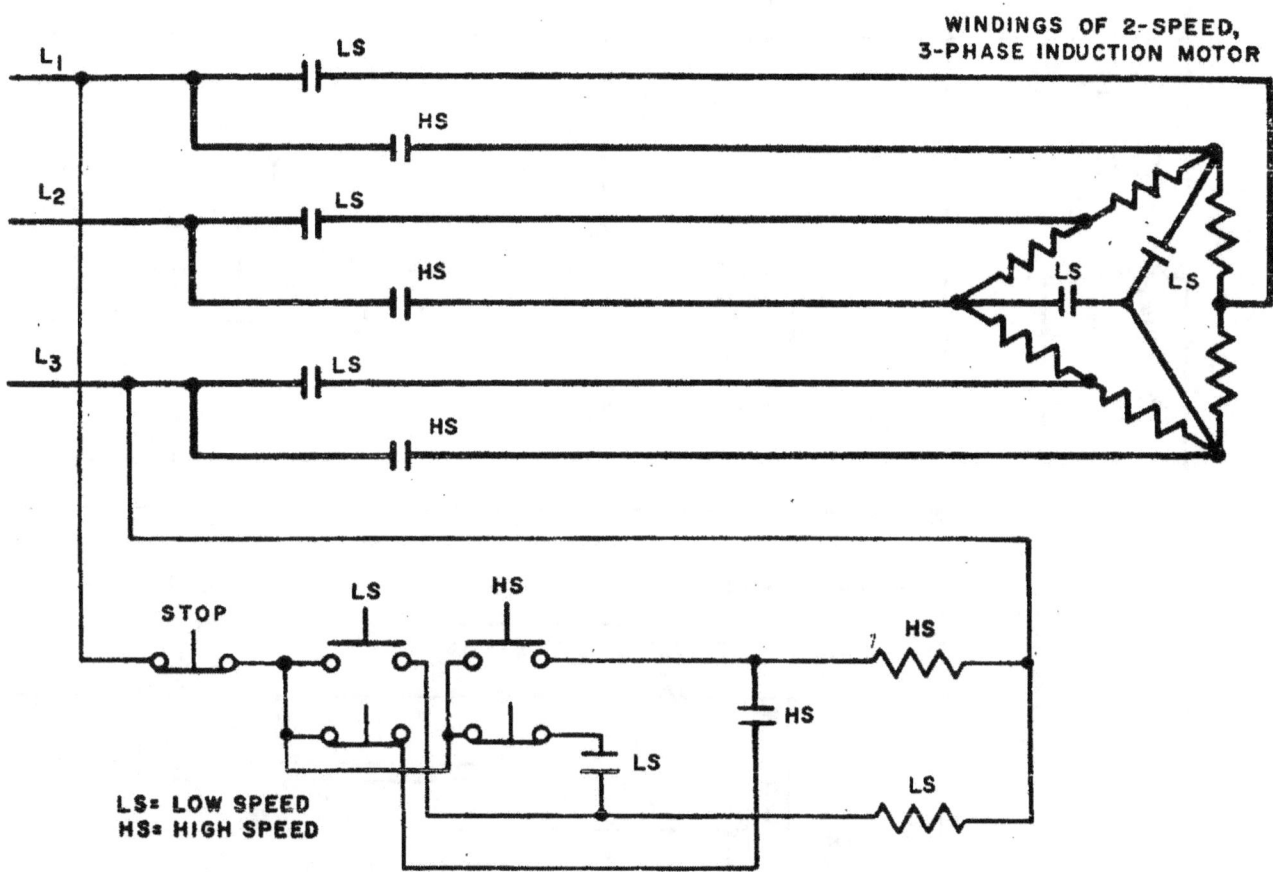

Figure C-39. An elementary schematic wiring diagram of an ac multispeed controller.

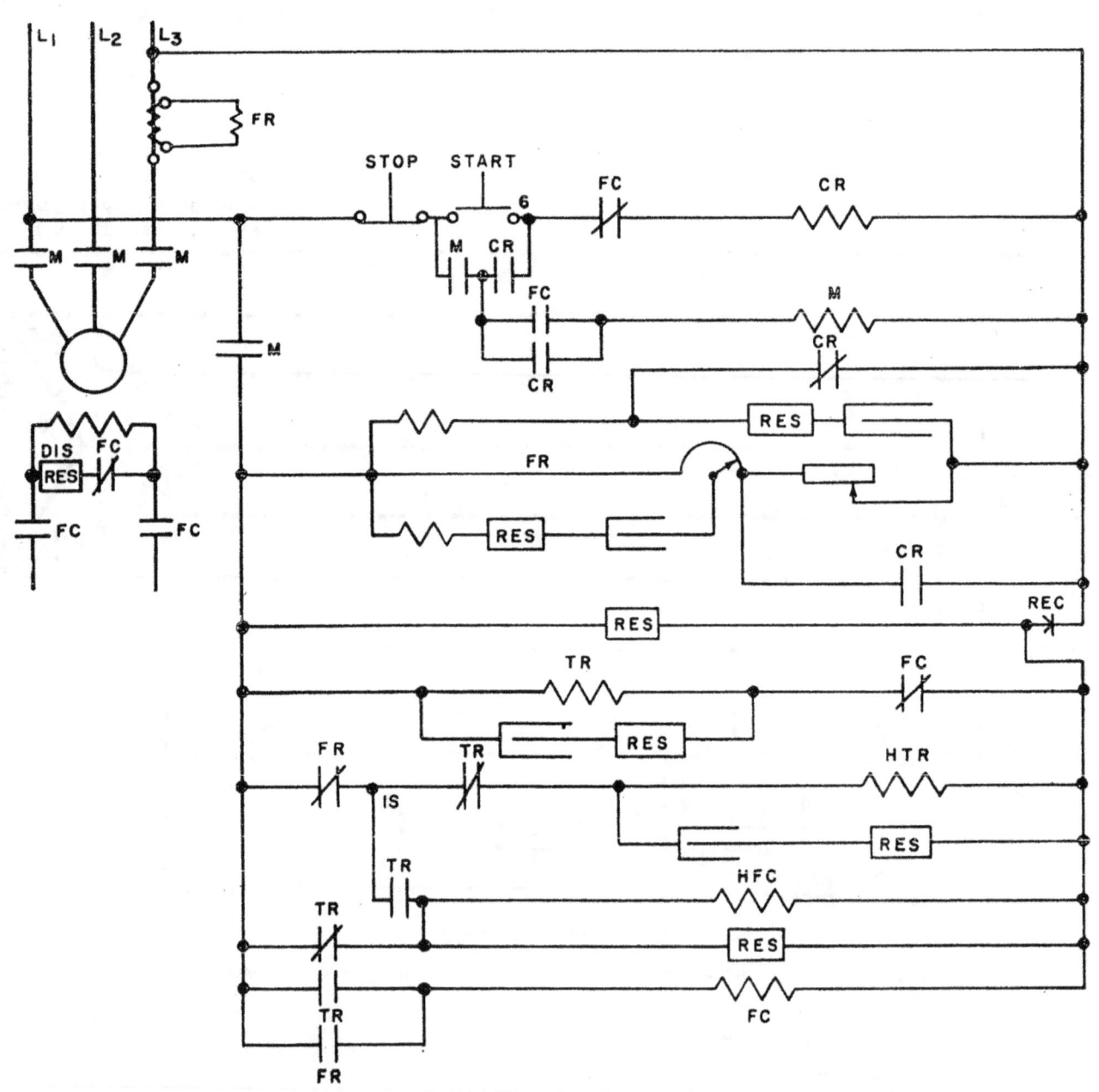

Figure C-40. An elementary schematic wiring diagram of a synchronous motor controller.

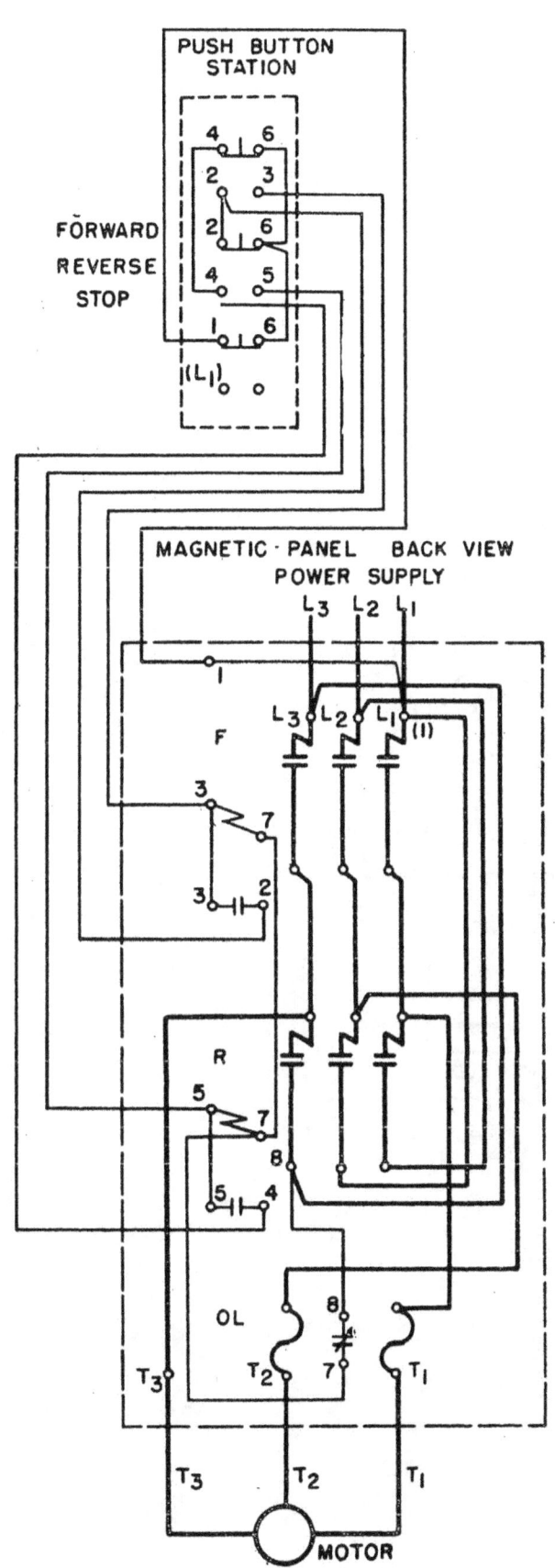

Figure C–41. A wiring diagram of a controller for an ac motor.

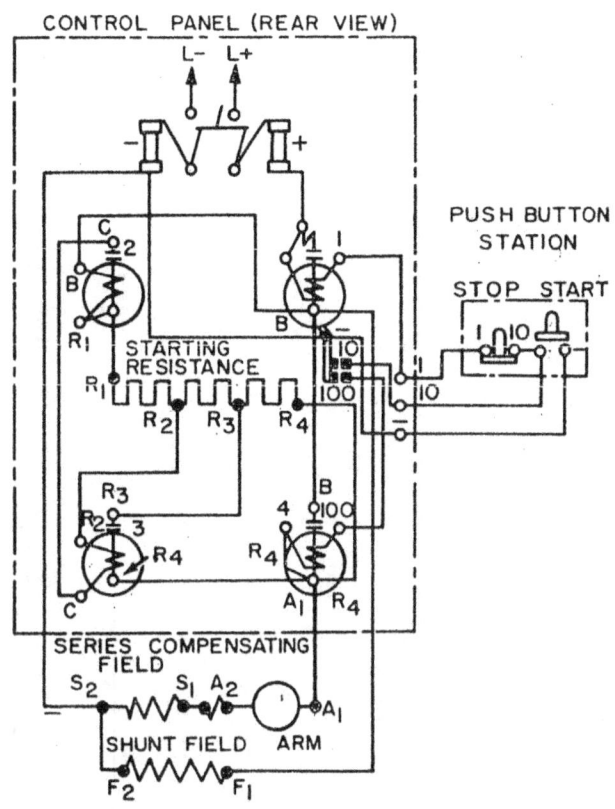

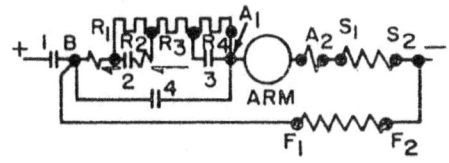

Figure C–42. A wiring diagram of a controller with three starting steps for a dc motor.

105

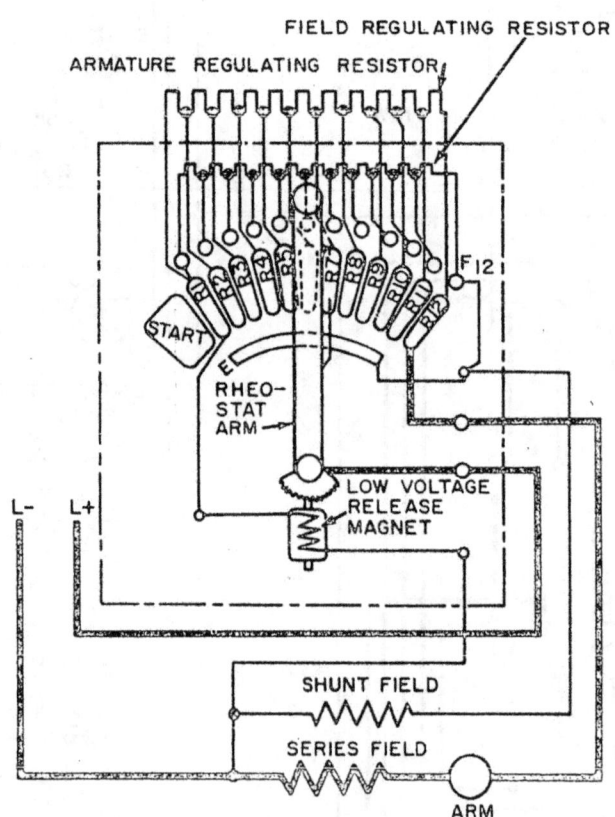

Figure C-43. A starting and speed-regulating rheostat having both armature and field resistors.

ELECTRICAL TERMS AND FORMULAS

CONTENTS

	Page
TERMS	1
Agonic ...... Dielectric	1
Diode ...... Lead	2
Line of Force ...... Resistor	3
Retentivity ...... Wattmeter	4
FORMULAS	4
Ohm's Law for D-C Circuits	4
Resistors in Series	4
Resistors in Parallel	4
R-L Circuit Time Constant	5
R-C Circuit Time Constant	5
Comparison of Units in Electric and Magnetic Circuits	5
Capacitors in Series	5
Capacitors in Parallel	5
Capacitive Reactance	5
Impedance in an R-C Circuit (Series)	5
Inductors in Series	5
Inductors in Parallel	5
Inductive Reactance	5
Q of a Coil	5
Impedance of an R-L Circuit (Series)	5
Impedance with R, C, and L in Series	5
Parallel Circuit Impedance	5
Sine-Wave Voltage Relationships	5
Power in A-C Circuit	6
Transformers	6
Three-Phase Voltage and Current Relationships	6
GREEK ALPHABET	7
Alpha ...... Omega	7
COMMON ABBREVIATIONS AND LETTER SYMBOLS	8
Alternating Current (noun) ...... Watt	8

ELECTRICAL TERMS AND FORMULAS

Terms

AGONIC.—An imaginary line of the earth's surface passing through points where the magnetic declination is 0°; that is, points where the compass points to true north.

AMMETER.—An instrument for measuring the amount of electron flow in amperes.

AMPERE.—The basic unit of electrical current.

AMPERE-TURN.—The magnetizing force produced by a current of one ampere flowing through a coil of one turn.

AMPLIDYNE.—A rotary magnetic or dynamoelectric amplifier used in servomechanism and control applications.

AMPLIFICATION.—The process of increasing the strength (current, power, or voltage) of a signal.

AMPLIFIER.—A device used to increase the signal voltage, current, or power, generally composed of a vacuum tube and associated circuit called a stage. It may contain several stages in order to obtain a desired gain.

AMPLITUDE.—The maximum instantaneous value of an alternating voltage or current, measured in either the positive or negative direction.

ARC.—A flash caused by an electric current ionizing a gas or vapor.

ARMATURE.—The rotating part of an electric motor or generator. The moving part of a relay or vibrator.

ATTENUATOR.—A network of resistors used to reduce voltage, current, or power delivered to a load.

AUTOTRANSFORMER.—A transformer in which the primary and secondary are connected together in one winding.

BATTERY.—Two or more primary or secondary cells connected together electrically. The term does not apply to a single cell.

BREAKER POINTS.—Metal contacts that open and close a circuit at timed intervals.

BRIDGE CIRCUIT.—The electrical bridge circuit is a term referring to any one of a variety of electric circuit networks, one branch of which, the "bridge" proper, connects two points of equal potential and hence carries no current when the circuit is properly adjusted or balanced.

BRUSH.—The conducting material, usually a block of carbon, bearing against the commutator or sliprings through which the current flows in or out.

BUS BAR.—A primary power distribution point connected to the main power source.

CAPACITOR.—Two electrodes or sets of electrodes in the form of plates, separated from each other by an insulating material called the dielectric.

CHOKE COIL.—A coil of low ohmic resistance and high impedance to alternating current.

CIRCUIT.—The complete path of an electric current.

CIRCUIT BREAKER.—An electromagnetic or thermal device that opens a circuit when the current in the circuit exceeds a predetermined amount. Circuit breakers can be reset.

CIRCULAR MIL.—An area equal to that of a circle with a diameter of 0.001 inch. It is used for measuring the cross section of wires.

COAXIAL CABLE.—A transmission line consisting of two conductors concentric with and insulated from each other.

COMMUTATOR.—The copper segments on the armature of a motor or generator. It is cylindrical in shape and is used to pass power into or from the brushes. It is a switching device.

CONDUCTANCE.—The ability of a material to conduct or carry an electric current. It is the reciprocal of the resistance of the material, and is expressed in mhos.

CONDUCTIVITY.—The ease with which a substance transmits electricity.

CONDUCTOR.—Any material suitable for carrying electric current.

CORE.—A magnetic material that affords an easy path for magnetic flux lines in a coil.

COUNTER E.M.F.—Counter electromotive force; an e.m.f. induced in a coil or armature that opposes the applied voltage.

CURRENT LIMITER.—A protective device similar to a fuse, usually used in high amperage circuits.

CYCLE.—One complete positive and one complete negative alternation of a current or voltage.

DIELECTRIC.—An insulator; a term that refers to the insulating material between the plates of a capacitor.

ELECTRICAL TERMS AND FORMULAS

DIODE.—Vacuum tube—a two element tube that contains a cathode and plate; semiconductor—a material of either germanium or silicon that is manufactured to allow current to flow in only one direction. Diodes are used as rectifiers and detectors.

DIRECT CURRENT.—An electric current that flows in one direction only.

EDDY CURRENT.—Induced circulating currents in a conducting material that are caused by a varying magnetic field.

EFFICIENCY.—The ratio of output power to input power, generally expressed as a percentage.

ELECTROLYTE.—A solution of a substance which is capable of conducting electricity. An electrolyte may be in the form of either a liquid or a paste.

ELECTROMAGNET.—A magnet made by passing current through a coil of wire wound on a soft iron core.

ELECTROMOTIVE FORCE (e.m.f.).—The force that produces an electric current in a circuit.

ELECTRON.—A negatively charged particle of matter.

ENERGY.—The ability or capacity to do work.

FARAD.—The unit of capacitance.

FEEDBACK.—A transfer of energy from the output circuit of a device back to its input.

FIELD.—The space containing electric or magnetic lines of force.

FIELD WINDING.—The coil used to provide the magnetizing force in motors and generators.

FLUX FIELD.—All electric or magnetic lines of force in a given region.

FREE ELECTRONS.—Electrons which are loosely held and consequently tend to move at random among the atoms of the material.

FREQUENCY.—The number of complete cycles per second existing in any form of wave motion; such as the number of cycles per second of an alternating current.

FULL-WAVE RECTIFIER CIRCUIT.—A circuit which utilizes both the positive and the negative alternations of an alternating current to produce a direct current.

FUSE.—A protective device inserted in series with a circuit. It contains a metal that will melt or break when current is increased beyond a specific value for a definite period of time.

GAIN.—The ratio of the output power, voltage, or current to the input power, voltage, or current, respectively.

GALVANOMETER.—An instrument used to measure small d-c currents.

GENERATOR.—A machine that converts mechanical energy into electrical energy.

GROUND.—A metallic connection with the earth to establish ground potential. Also, a common return to a point of zero potential. The chassis of a receiver or a transmitter is sometimes the common return, and therefore the ground of the unit.

HENRY.—The basic unit of inductance.

HORSEPOWER.—The English unit of power, equal to work done at the rate of 550 foot-pounds per second. Equal to 746 watts of electrical power.

HYSTERESIS.—A lagging of the magnetic flux in a magnetic material behind the magnetizing force which is producing it.

IMPEDANCE.—The total opposition offered to the flow of an alternating current. It may consist of any combination of resistance, inductive reactance, and capacitive reactance.

INDUCTANCE.—The property of a circuit which tends to oppose a change in the existing current.

INDUCTION.—The act or process of producing voltage by the relative motion of a magnetic field across a conductor.

INDUCTIVE REACTANCE.—The opposition to the flow of alternating or pulsating current caused by the inductance of a circuit. It is measured in ohms.

INPHASE.—Applied to the condition that exists when two waves of the same frequency pass through their maximum and minimum values of like polarity at the same instant.

INVERSELY.—Inverted or reversed in position or relationship.

ISOGONIC LINE.—An imaginary line drawn through points on the earth's surface where the magnetic deviation is equal.

JOULE.—A unit of energy or work. A joule of energy is liberated by one ampere flowing for one second through a resistance of one ohm.

KILO.—A prefix meaning 1,000.

LAG.—The amount one wave is behind another in time; expressed in electrical degrees.

LAMINATED CORE.—A core built up from thin sheets of metal and used in transformers and relays.

LEAD.—The opposite of LAG. Also, a wire or connection.

ELECTRICAL TERMS AND FORMULAS

LINE OF FORCE.—A line in an electric or magnetic field that shows the direction of the force.

LOAD.—The power that is being delivered by any power producing device. The equipment that uses the power from the power producing device.

MAGNETIC AMPLIFIER.—A saturable reactor type device that is used in a circuit to amplify or control.

MAGNETIC CIRCUIT.—The complete path of magnetic lines of force.

MAGNETIC FIELD.—The space in which a magnetic force exists.

MAGNETIC FLUX.—The total number of lines of force issuing from a pole of a magnet.

MAGNETIZE.—To convert a material into a magnet by causing the molecules to rearrange.

MAGNETO.—A generator which produces alternating current and has a permanent magnet as its field.

MEGGER.—A test instrument used to measure insulation resistance and other high resistances. It is a portable hand operated d-c generator used as an ohmmeter.

MEGOHM.—A million ohms.

MICRO.—A prefix meaning one-millionth.

MILLI.—A prefix meaning one-thousandth.

MILLIAMMETER.—An ammeter that measures current in thousandths of an ampere.

MOTOR-GENERATOR.—A motor and a generator with a common shaft used to convert line voltages to other voltages or frequencies.

MUTUAL INDUCTANCE.—A circuit property existing when the relative position of two inductors causes the magnetic lines of force from one to link with the turns of the other.

NEGATIVE CHARGE.—The electrical charge carried by a body which has an excess of electrons.

NEUTRON.—A particle having the weight of a proton but carrying no electric charge. It is located in the nucleus of an atom.

NUCLEUS.—The central part of an atom that is mainly comprised of protons and neutrons. It is the part of the atom that has the most mass.

NULL.—Zero.

OHM.—The unit of electrical resistance.

OHMMETER.—An instrument for directly measuring resistance in ohms.

OVERLOAD.—A load greater than the rated load of an electrical device.

PERMALLOY.—An alloy of nickel and iron having an abnormally high magnetic permeability.

PERMEABILITY.—A measure of the ease with which magnetic lines of force can flow through a material as compared to air.

PHASE DIFFERENCE.—The time in electrical degrees by which one wave leads or lags another.

POLARITY.—The character of having magnetic poles, or electric charges.

POLE.—The section of a magnet where the flux lines are concentrated; also where they enter and leave the magnet. An electrode of a battery.

POLYPHASE.—A circuit that utilizes more than one phase of alternating current.

POSITIVE CHARGE.—The electrical charge carried by a body which has become deficient in electrons.

POTENTIAL.—The amount of charge held by a body as compared to another point or body. Usually measured in volts.

POTENTIOMETER.—A variable voltage divider; a resistor which has a variable contact arm so that any portion of the potential applied between its ends may be selected.

POWER.—The rate of doing work or the rate of expending energy. The unit of electrical power is the watt.

POWER FACTOR.—The ratio of the actual power of an alternating or pulsating current, as measured by a wattmeter, to the apparent power, as indicated by ammeter and voltmeter readings. The power factor of an inductor, capacitor, or insulator is an expression of their losses.

PRIME MOVER.—The source of mechanical power used to drive the rotor of a generator.

PROTON.—A positively charged particle in the nucleus of an atom.

RATIO.—The value obtained by dividing one number by another, indicating their relative proportions.

REACTANCE.—The opposition offered to the flow of an alternating current by the inductance, capacitance, or both, in any circuit.

RECTIFIERS.—Devices used to change alternating current to unidirectional current. These may be vacuum tubes, semiconductors such as germanium and silicon, and dry-disk rectifiers such as selenium and copper-oxide.

RELAY.—An electromechanical switching device that can be used as a remote control.

RELUCTANCE.—A measure of the opposition that a material offers to magnetic lines of force.

RESISTANCE.—The opposition to the flow of current caused by the nature and physical dimensions of a conductor.

RESISTOR.—A circuit element whose chief characteristic is resistance; used to oppose the flow of current.

ELECTRICAL TERMS AND FORMULAS

RETENTIVITY.—The measure of the ability of a material to hold its magnetism.

RHEOSTAT.—A variable resistor.

SATURABLE REACTOR.—A control device that uses a small d-c current to control a large a-c current by controlling core flux density.

SATURATION.—The condition existing in any circuit when an increase in the driving signal produces no further change in the resultant effect.

SELF-INDUCTION.—The process by which a circuit induces an e.m.f. into itself by its own magnetic field.

SERIES-WOUND.—A motor or generator in which the armature is wired in series with the field winding.

SERVO.—A device used to convert a small movement into one of greater movement or force.

SERVOMECHANISM.—A closed-loop system that produces a force to position an object in accordance with the information that originates at the input.

SOLENOID.—An electromagnetic coil that contains a movable plunger.

SPACE CHARGE.—The cloud of electrons existing in the space between the cathode and plate in a vacuum tube, formed by the electrons emitted from the cathode in excess of those immediately attracted to the plate.

SPECIFIC GRAVITY—The ratio between the density of a substance and that of pure water, at a given temperature.

SYNCHROSCOPE—An instrument used to indicate a difference in frequency between two a-c sources.

SYNCHRO SYSTEM.—An electrical system that gives remote indications or control by means of self-synchronizing motors.

TACHOMETER.—An instrument for indicating revolutions per minute.

TERTIARY WINDING.—A third winding on a transformer or magnetic amplifier that is used as a second control winding.

THERMISTOR.—A resistor that is used to compensate for temperature variations in a circuit.

THERMOCOUPLE.—A junction of two dissimilar metals that produces a voltage when heated.

TORQUE.—The turning effort or twist which a shaft sustains when transmitting power.

TRANSFORMER.—A device composed of two or more coils, linked by magnetic lines of force, used to transfer energy from one circuit to another.

TRANSMISSION LINES.—Any conductor or system of conductors used to carry electrical energy from its source to a load.

VARS.—Abbreviation for volt-ampere, reactive.

VECTOR.—A line used to represent both direction and magnitude.

VOLT.—The unit of electrical potential.

VOLTMETER.—An instrument designed to measure a difference in electrical potential, in volts.

WATT.—The unit of electrical power.

WATTMETER.—An instrument for measuring electrical power in watts.

Formulas

Ohm's Law for d-c Circuits

$$I = \frac{E}{R} = \frac{P}{E} = \sqrt{\frac{P}{R}}$$

$$R = \frac{E}{I} = \frac{P}{I^2} = \frac{E^2}{P}$$

$$E = IR = \frac{P}{I} = \sqrt{PR}$$

$$P = EI = \frac{E^2}{R} = I^2 R$$

Resistors in Series

$$R_T = R_1 + R_2 \ldots$$

Resistors in Parallel
Two resistors

$$R_T = \frac{R_1 R_2}{R_1 + R_2}$$

More than two

$$\frac{1}{R_T} = \frac{1}{R_1} + \frac{1}{R_2} + \frac{1}{R_3}$$

ELECTRICAL TERMS AND FORMULAS

R-L Circuit Time Constant equals

$$\frac{L \text{ (in henrys)}}{R \text{ (in ohms)}} = t \text{ (in seconds)}, \text{ or}$$

$$\frac{L \text{ (in microhenrys)}}{R \text{ (in ohms)}} = t \text{ (in microseconds)}$$

R-C Circuit Time Constant equals
R (ohms) X C (farads) = t (seconds)
R (megohms) x C (microfarads) = t (seconds)
R (ohms) x C (microfarads) = t (microseconds)
R (megohms) x C (micromicrofrads) = t (microseconds)

Comparison of Units in Electric and Magnetic Circuits.

	Electric circuit	Magnetic circuit
Force	Volt, E or e.m.f.	Gilberts, F, or m.m.f.
Flow	Ampere, I	Flux, Φ, in maxwells
Opposition	Ohms, R	Reluctance, R
Law	Ohm's law, $I = \frac{E}{R}$	Rowland's law $\Phi = \frac{F}{R}$
Intensity of force	Volts per cm. of length	$H = \frac{1.257 IN}{L}$, gilberts per centimeter of length
Density	Current density — for example, amperes per cm^2.	Flux density — for example, lines per cm^2., or gausses

Capacitors in Series
Two capacitors

$$C_T = \frac{C_1 C_2}{C_1 + C_2}$$

More than two

$$\frac{1}{C_T} = \frac{1}{C_1} + \frac{1}{C_2} + \frac{1}{C_3} \ldots$$

Capacitors in Parallel

$$C_T = C_1 + C_2 \ldots$$

Capacitive Reactance

$$X_c = \frac{1}{2\pi f C}$$

Impedance in an R-C Circuit (Series)

$$Z = \sqrt{R^2 + X_c^2}$$

Inductors in Series

$$L_T = L_1 + L_2 \ldots \text{ (No coupling between coils)}$$

Inductors in Parallel
Two inductors

$$L_T = \frac{L_1 L_2}{L_1 + L_2} \text{ (No coupling between coils)}$$

More than two

$$\frac{1}{L_T} = \frac{1}{L_1} + \frac{1}{L_2} + \frac{1}{L_3} \ldots \text{ (No coupling between coils)}$$

Inductive Reactance

$$X_L = 2\pi f L$$

Q of a Coil

$$Q = \frac{X_L}{R}$$

Impedance of an R-L Circuit (series)

$$Z = \sqrt{R^2 + X_L^2}$$

Impedance with R, C, and L in Series

$$Z = \sqrt{R^2 + (X_L - X_C)^2}$$

Parallel Circuit Impedance

$$Z = \frac{Z_1 Z_2}{Z_1 + Z_2}$$

Sine-Wave Voltage Relationships
Average value

$$E_{ave} = \frac{2}{\pi} \times E_{max} = 0.637 E_{max}$$

ELECTRICAL TERMS AND FORMULAS

Effective or r.m.s. value

$$E_{eff} = \frac{E_{max}}{\sqrt{2}} = \frac{E_{max}}{1.414} = 0.707 E_{max} = 1.11 E_{ave}$$

Maximum value

$$E_{max} = \sqrt{2} E_{eff} = 1.414 E_{eff} = 1.57 E_{ave}$$

Voltage in an a-c circuit

$$E = IZ = \frac{P}{I \times P.F.}$$

Current in an a-c circuit

$$I = \frac{E}{Z} = \frac{P}{E \times P.F.}$$

Power in A-C Circuit
Apparent power $= EI$
True power

$$P = EI \cos\theta = EI \times P.F.$$

Power factor

$$P.F. = \frac{P}{EI} = \cos\theta$$

$$\cos\theta = \frac{\text{true power}}{\text{apparent power}}$$

Transformers
Voltage relationship

$$\frac{E}{E} = \frac{N}{N} \text{ or } E = E \times \frac{N}{N}$$

Current relationship

$$\frac{I_p}{I_s} = \frac{N_s}{N_p}$$

Induced voltage

$$E_{eff} = 4.44 \, BAfN 10^{-8}$$

Turns ratio equals

$$\frac{N_p}{N_s} = \sqrt{\frac{Z_p}{Z_s}}$$

Secondary current

$$I_s = I_p \frac{N_p}{N_s}$$

Secondary voltage

$$E_s = E_p \frac{N_s}{N_p}$$

Three Phase Voltage and Current Relationships
With wye connected windings

$$E_{line} = 1.732 E_{coil} = \sqrt{3} E_{coil}$$

$$I_{line} = I_{coil}$$

With delta connected windings

$$E_{line} = E_{coil}$$

$$I_{line} = 1.732 I_{coil}$$

With wye or delta connected winding

$$P_{coil} = E_{coil} I_{coil}$$

$$P_t = 3 P_{coil}$$

$$P_t = 1.732 E_{line} I_{line}$$

(To convert to true power multiply by $\cos\theta$)

Synchronous Speed of Motor

$$r.p.m. = \frac{120 \times \text{frequency}}{\text{number of poles}}$$

GREEK ALPHABET

Name	Capital	Lower Case	Designates
Alpha	A	α	Angles.
Beta	B	β	Angles, flux density.
Gamma ...	Γ	γ	Conductivity.
Delta	Δ	δ	Variation of a quantity, increment.
Epsilon ...	E	ε	Base of natural logarithms (2.71828).
Zeta	Z	ζ	Impedance, coefficients, coordinates.
Eta	H	η	Hysteresis coefficient, efficiency, magnetizing force.
Theta	Θ	θ	Phase angle.
Iota	I	ι	
Kappa	K	κ	Dielectric constant, coupling coefficient, susceptibility.
Lambda ...	Λ	λ	Wavelength.
Mu	M	μ	Permeability, micro, amplification factor.
Nu	N	ν	Reluctivity.
Xi	Ξ	ξ	
Omicron ...	O	o	
Pi	Π	π	3.1416
Rho	P	ρ	Resistivity.
Sigma	Σ	σ	
Tau	T	τ	Time constant, time-phase displacement.
Upsilon ...	Υ	υ	
Phi	Φ	φ	Angles, magnetic flux.
Chi	X	χ	
Psi	Ψ	ψ	Dielectric flux, phase difference.
Omega	Ω	ω	Ohms (capital), angular velocity ($2\pi f$).

COMMON ABBREVIATIONS AND LETTER SYMBOLS

Term	Abbreviation or Symbol
alternating current (noun)	a.c.
alternating-current (adj.)	a-c
ampere	a.
area	A
audiofrequency (noun)	AF
audiofrequency (adj.)	A-F
capacitance	C
capacitive reactance	X_C
centimeter	cm.
conductance	G
coulomb	Q
counterelectromotive force	c.e.m.f.
current (d-c or r.m.s. value)	I
current (instantaneous value)	i
cycles per second	c.p.s.
dielectric constant	K, k
difference in potential (d-c or r.m.s. value)	E
difference in potential (instantaneous value)	e
direct current (noun)	d.c.
direct-current (adj.)	d-c
electromotive force	e.m.f.
frequency	f
henry	h.
horsepower	hp.
impedance	Z
inductance	L
inductive reactance	X_L
kilovolt	kv.
kilovolt-ampere	kv.-a.
kilowatt	kw.
kilowatt-hour	kw.-hr.
magnetic field intensity	H
magnetomotive force	m.m.f.
megohm	M
microampere	μ a.
microfarad	μ f.
microhenry	μ h.
micromicrofarad	$\mu\mu$ f.
microvolt	μ v.
milliampere	ma.
millihenry	mh.
milliwatt	mw.
mutual inductance	M
power	P
resistance	R
revolutions per minute	r.p.m.
root mean square	r.m.s.
time	t
torque	T
volt	v.
watt	w.